B. S. *
AND LIVE LONGER

*BEAT STRESS

by Dr. Jim Keelan

Communications Unlimited
Arvada, Colorado

B. S. And Live Longer

Copyright© 1978 by James Keelan
Printed in the United States of America
All rights reserved
No part of this book may be used or
reproduced in any manner whatsoever
without written permission except
in the case of brief quotations
embodied in critical articles and
reviews. For further information, write
to the author, c/o Communications
Unlimited, 7057 Wright Court,
Arvada, Colorado 80004

Library of Congress Catalog Card Number: 78-61421

TABLE OF CONTENTS

INTRODUCTION
- Who is the author? — 1
- Where did the title come from? — 9
- What is the approach? — 11

CHAPTER I
- Why is stress the No. 1 killer in America? — 17

CHAPTER II
- What are the nuts and bolts of stress? — 21

CHAPTER III
- What makes the workaholic tick and his heart stop? — 25

CHAPTER IV
- What causes stress in the everyday person? — 33

CHAPTER V
- How do I score on the "Stress Assessment Test?" — 39

CHAPTER VI
- How does the everyday person reduce stress? — 47

CHAPTER VII
- What are your stress generators? — 53
  1. Do I have a philosophical stress generator? — 53
  2. Do I have a psychological stress generator? — 64
  3. Do I have a communicational stress generator? — 74
  4. Do I have a male-female hang-up stress generator? — 88
  5. Do I have a role-identity stress generator? — 94

CHAPTER VIII
- Where do I begin? — 103
- What are the 21 ways to cope with your principal stress generator? — 107

APPENDIX
- How can you reduce stress in students and children? — 151
- I Critical parent-child approach — 153
- II Nurturing parent-child approach — 161
- III Adult-adult approach — 164
- IV Child-child approach — 174
- V Does your "cope" runneth over with stress? — 176
- VI Changing the things you can change — 176

Dedicated to "Flexible Fran"
and Kevin and Kenny —
My Three Stress Reducers

FORWARD

Citizens of the United States are involved in an epidemic of coronary artery disease — a process of fat deposition in the coronary arteries which often ends in sudden death, heart attack, chest pain or heart failure. There are several factors which appear to increase the risk of developing coronary artery disease: high blood cholestrol, hypertension, cigarette smoking, diabetes, lack of exercise, advancing age, a strong family history of coronary artery disease, obesity, being male, and personality type. The importance of one's personality is that it determines how one responds to stress — if stress is not handled well and mechanisms for recognizing and dealing constructively with stresses are not identified, the person appears to be at a substantially higher risk for developing coronary disease than a more tranquil colleague. Actually, one doesn't need the increased risk of heart disease to justify a concerted effort to beat the effects of stress — the improved quality of day-to-day living is ample justification alone.

Stress is an inevitable part of living. Some of it is good, and in fact, may be necessary to optimize creative productivity and the quality of one's relationships with others. The compassionate, understanding and gently applied stressors bring out and help to maintain the best in all of us. The comment: "Well done! I'm sure glad I asked you to do that job. You accomplished a great deal under circumstances that I know were difficult for you." — creates a desire and determination (stress) to continue to improve job performance and sustain the mature relationship with the supervisor.

Unfortunately, we in the United States are usually subjected to more harsh, debilitating stress than to constructive stress. These stresses create anxiety, worry, and frustration. They compromise productivity and prevent quality living as we are unable to meet the demands applied by the stress for increased output, a higher level of accomplishment or a higher standard of living. It is often difficult, if not impossible to control the sources of external stress and thereby be relieved of the discomfort they cause. It is, on the other hand, not only desirable, but quite possible for one to learn to identify and ultimately control the sources of stress that come from within — the internal and individual attitudes and responses to external stress sources that we unwittingly harbor.

In his typically straightforward, humorous, candid, and conversational manner, Dr. Jim Keelan directs the reader through the process of recognizing personal stressors and doing something about them.

Jim Keelan observes life and its problems with insight, understanding, compassion and humor. His position is eternally optimistic: things **can** be better. Attention to the guidelines laid down in this book will prove that statement to the delight of the reader.

Dr. H. L. Brammell, M.D., Cardiologist
Associate Professor of Medicine,
Physical Medicine and Rehabilitation
University of Colorado Medical Center
Director of Rehabilitation
Research and Training Center

ACKNOWLEDGMENTS

My thanks for the most productive drink in the bar at the Holiday Inn in Oklahoma City, which is where this book all began. I just had finished the first day of my "Listening to Self" workshop. Ray Savera, then a Colonel in the Air Force, bought me a drink. The drink lasted from 4:00 in the afternoon until midnight. He told me, "Your stuff is a 'shoe-in' for stress reduction, and is severely needed in the Air Force." During our lengthy discussion, we outlined "Managerial Communication and Stress Reduction" for the Air Force. Since then, I've given Stress Management workshops to people in the Armed Services, business, government, and education, including three trips to Hawaii for Stress Reduction seminars. Special thanks to Ray (now in personnel with McDonald's Hamburgers) for buying me the most powerful drink in my career.

Thanks to John Roughan, my long-time buddy. Our long talks in Hawaii were essential for getting it all together. Thanks to Annie Patrick, my colleague at Communication Unlimited, who kept saying, "You gotta get that book done." Thanks to Dee Schneider, who typed faster than I could think, and who gave me immediate and helpful feedback as she typed. Thanks to my good friend Marilyn Shippman, who gave me the caterpillar idea. Thanks to Gary Giann, who forced "all the irons" into this book, coordinating production and printing. Thanks to the free art contributed by my boys Kevin and Kenny. Thanks to Susan Novak, whose art makes the message jump out at you. Thanks to the many everyday people who shared their stresses and their lives so that the message of this book could come alive in your life. Thanks to all I should have mentioned by name, but have forgotten.

Finally, thanks to my wife, "Flexible Fran", who helps to form the vital links in our relationship which give us room to be ourselves. A part of being myself is writing this book so others can hopefully "Beat Stress and Live Fuller and Longer".

ideas
ideas
IDEAS
ideas
IDEAS
ideas
IDEAS
IDEAS
ideas
ideas
ideas
ideas
ideas
IDEAS

INTRODUCTION

Experts are finally saying what many of us everyday folks have known all along. "Too much stress will drive you to the grave or to the nearest mental institution." The goal of this book is to help the reader avoid both of those paths by providing relevant coping tools which can create a sound mind in a healthy body. Actually, the goal, in more vivid words, is to "make butterflies out of caterpillars".

Who wrote this book?

In 1948, I met John Roughan at the Marist Seminary in Penndel, Pennsylvania. We were both in our second year of college. Since then we have become the best of friends with a lot in common. We both are former priests, married, and now are real "fathers". We studied years of philosophy and psychology together, and spent lots of stimulating moments tossing the ideas in this book back and forth in the relaxing atmosphere of Hawaii.

Although the words are mine, the philosphy of this book is a combination of the ideas of both of us. I've had such good feedback on "Introducing Myself" in my first book, **Having Fun Being Yourself**, that I am going to repeat it for the new reader. Basically I "talk a book". I see it as a rap session between you and me. It makes sense to know with whom you are talking, so I'll introduce myself, just as I did in **Having Fun Being Yourself**. For those of you who know me, just skip the next few pages.

Who am I and who are you?

In September of 1970, I started the doctoral program at the University of Northern Colorado, thanks to a graduate assistantship. I enrolled in a class in Humanistic Psychology and "lo and behold" the teacher took the first hour or so of class to share his background. He happened to become the best psychology teacher I have ever had — and maybe sharing his humanness was a big part of it. He never put himself above anyone. He, too, was just a member of the human race. For me this was a "peak experience" in learning in the field of education. Looking back I see that 26 years of my life (more than half my life) was spent in school. Dick Usher was the first teacher who took time out to share himself as a person with the class. Later I found it was more than just chance. He had done research to find out that the most effective tool of the teacher is not his writings, his intelligence, his degrees, but himself. It actually is the person of the teacher and the atmosphere he sets that produces an ideal or stress-filled learning environment. At any rate, I was so impressed with Dick's personalistic approach, that I have adopted it. Before every class, every workshop, I take time to share a little bit about "who am I?" Hopefully, you'll get more from this book if you know a little bit about me.

Who am I?

In January of 1930, I appeared on the scene. My dad is as Irish as a four leaf clover and my mother is a warm people-person German. I grew up in North Denver — known as a rough-tough part of town. Like a lot of kids I played the role of a tough guy and an Athlete (known as "Jocks" by today's generation). The series of events in my life point out the fact that my life was definitely determined by my values. I valued the role of being tough, and I was.

A ride in the laundry truck

Actually we didn't get into too much trouble with the law. However, one night we, my brother Joe and I plus our Italian friends, Tony and Pat, were playing cards when Billy, an eighth grade drop-out, honked the horn outside. "How about going for a ride?" he shouted. We jumped in to find (several blocks later) that he had stolen the Capitol Laundry truck that we were riding in. We all played the "I'm not chicken" role and spent the next several hours taking turns driving. However, on our way home about 11:00 p.m. two police cars pulled us over. Tony and I quietly tried to sneak out the back door until the policeman grabbed us with the words, "Where are you going?" We replied, "It's such a nice evening, officer, that we thought we'd take a walk." Incidentally, Tony is now a juvenile officer. This was his inservice training.

At the police station we were waiting for questioning which we called the third degree. One policeman gave us some chewing gum and we thought that he was really cool. They took my brother Joe first. They asked him where he was at a certain date, and implied that he might have stolen some things from a filling station. They picked the wrong man. Joe could out-talk anyone. Very indignantly he gave the questioners a lecture after they called him a liar. "Do you realize that I am not only a Catholic at St. Pat's School, but an altar boy — and altar boys don't lie — dammit." Joe wore them out so that we didn't get questioned at all.

The best altar boys

They took us to the "Holiday Inn" as I like to call it. Others called it the detention home. It was a little scary, but it certainly was a learning experience. The next day was December 8, 1943, the Feast of the Immaculate Conception, a big day in the Catholic Church. However, Fr. Barry, the Irish priest at St. Pat's, had no altar boys for the 7:00 a.m. Mass. They were all in jail. In no time, Fr. Barry was down at the detention home. He told them: "You can't keep these boys here — they are me best altar boys." I often wondered what they thought his worst ones were like. He said, "Jimmie, me lad, did ya steal the truck?" "No, Father," I replied. "Okay, give the keys back and let's go," said he. On December 8th, we were sprung. For two weeks my classmates wouldn't talk to me because their parents told them to stay away from Jimmy "cause he steals cars." Later I broke the role barrier of a car thief.

Football and no. 1

Just like today, we wanted to be number one in football. As a result, we traveled across town to St. Joe's, known for its championship football teams. The blood, sweat, and tears that went into football practice were living proof that being a championship football team was a major value in our lives. Since then I have changed values, but at that time my value for football enabled me to take a lot of knocks physically.

Parties or studies

Studying really wasn't a big value in our gang. First of all, if I had brought a book home I might have endangered my role of a tough guy and could have been classified as an "egg head" — a title I didn't want. Secondly, I really was content to just coast by in school with a minimum of effort spiced with a little copying when the answers were really tough.

The time we didn't use in studies released us for more interesting endeavors like parties, jitter-bugging, hotrods, and drinking beer. Our motivation grew with each party. My high school chum, named Buddy, was a real fun-loving guy. Neither of us was a candidate for the National Honor Society, but both of us really enjoyed high school (although we were considered the most likely not to succeed). We kept our minds active in school by planning and executing intricate practical jokes. We never got caught, but one joke had a reverse effect.

The joke that backfired

It was graduation year — 1947. Buddy said, "Let's play a joke on the gang." I replied, "Impossible, they know us too well." He said that it would work because he figured it all out. Everyone was talking about their plans for after graduation. All we had to do was to think of something different and tell them that we were going into that field. We thought and thought. The craziest idea that we could come up with was to tell them that we wanted to be like Fr. Schwartz, our athletic director, an ex-football player who became a priest. Leaving a career in football to become a priest was like going from a GS-17 in the government to a GS-1. From our teenager value system, we looked at anyone who went to the "Priest Factory" as someone who couldn't find anyone to marry and just couldn't hack it in the world. It really seemed like an "out of sight" idea. After a party, Buddy sprang the news on the gang. They rolled in the aisles. One gal named Pat said, "My God, if you and Jimmy become priests, I'm going to become a nun." Well, of all the gang, she was in no way headed in that direction.

The seminarians

For some it was so funny, that they called us the seminarians. On our way out of school for a three day suspension, someone remarked, "Aren't the seminarians supposed to give good examples?" The gang didn't fall for the joke, but it did work. Fr. Barry, the priest who sprang us from the detention home, was transferred, and in came Fr. Haas who was really interested in athletics. At one of the games he overheard someone say, "Jimmy, our seminarian, made a touchdown." The next day he was at my door just as enthused as a kid with his first bike. "I hear that you are going to the seminary," he said. I really didn't know how to respond. First of all, it was usually the police department and not the priest at my door. I asked him where he'd heard that. I knew that he'd fallen for the joke, but I wasn't about to tell him that Buddy and I thought that being priests would be the most idiotic thing we could do. I finally decided to play along and hoped he would forget about it. However, he came out regularly and took me for coffee and doughnuts, games, picnics, etc. I told Buddy. He laughed and asked, "Why don't you tell the poor guy?" I told him, "You're crazy, Buddy, I'll keep up the free treats he gives me. I'll tell him in June when I get another job somewhere. This is real North Denver Diplomacy." In June I told him that I had a nice job and changed my mind. He accepted it graciously. That was the end of the "free-bees," but my diplomacy worked.

The New Amsterdam Casualty Company

I was offered a job at the New Amsterdam Insurance Company because they wanted a male typist. Buddy and I decided to join the typing class because there were forty girls in the class and they looked lonely. Buddy had a short attention span — and got kicked out. I kept my eyes on the keys and the girls at the same time and made it. So there I was at the insurance company. At best I could type 16 words a minute with 15 mistakes. I later became the greatest casualty that they ever had by mis-filing many of their policies. They hadn't asked me if I knew the alphabet before giving me some filing duties.

The negative counselor

I had never met a counselor. I had learned to type and so ended up in an insurance company. Certainly it was not a planned vocation. However, I feel that we can learn from good experiences as well as from bummers. My negative counselor, an insurance agent, was a real bummer. He thought that there were four persons in God, and he was the fourth person. He played such a superior role that I felt like sliding him down the linen chute. However, he occasioned my first four real thoughts in life (I went through school with a perfect record — no thoughts).

The joke backfired

After an encounter with this agent, I had my first four

significant thoughts. It was the last of August and football was in the air. My first thought was depressing — no more football — I graduated. My second thought was, "I guess that I'm going to be in insurance." My third one was, "If I stay here, eventually I'll become an insurance agent like the phony agent that irritates me." I said to myself, "In no way." So I quit. Then I thought of Fr. Haas whom I had gotten to know by accident. I said, "He isn't a phony. He's neat. He's always around sports. He likes kids. I like sports. I like kids. Therefore, I am going to be a priest."

She locked the kitchen door

That very day I went home to tell my mother. She locked the kitchen door and said, "Sshh . . . I won't tell anyone. If this is another joke, tell me." I really couldn't blame my mom because of my infamous background of joking. I told her that I was going to give it a try because of that phony insurance agent. I mentioned that if I liked it, I'd stay. If not, I'd quit. The next day I told my girlfriend. Needless to say, that didn't set too well because I'm sure that she planned to be in the ring race of '47. At that time a girl was an old maid if she was single at 19. However, she was married in several months. She was good looking and well built — my value system at that time. Thank God that we didn't get married, because we were so temperamentally different that it just wouldn't have lasted.

A verb from a vegetable

I took the entrance exam for the seminary. I flunked the English part. I was angry and surprised. I told them, "English is my best subject — I talk it all the time." However, I had to go to Regis College a year to make up the English. I really didn't know a verb from a vegetable. After a year I learned enough to get into the seminary.

I studied for three months. Then I smuggled a squirt gun into the room. I shot my roommates. Soon they had one in self-defense. Then we went to other rooms during study periods. Sometimes it ended by throwing buckets of water. I got more interested in jokes than studying and my grades went down proportionately. I quit at the end of the year before they could kick me out. I was back with the old gang and Buddy. Both of our girlfriends were in nurses' training. I forgot about the seminary when a new parish priest, Fr. McGuire, came out and talked me into trying out in the Marists, a religious educational order. He got me interested by telling me that they were good athletes. I gave them a chance. I spent one year in Pennsylvania, one year in New York, two years in Boston, and four years in Washington, D.C. In 1957 I made it.

Pope in four years

I returned to Denver, and neighbors asked, "Jimmy, are you really a priest? What's happened to the Catholic Church?" I told them that I would be Pope in four years. I never reached my goal. I was assigned to San Rafael, California, where I coached football, basketball, and baseball. Among other things, I also taught English. It wasn't too long after that when they asked how I would like to go to a parish. Where? Hawaii. I said, "I'll take it."

I loved Hawaii. I was assistant pastor in charge of youth. I loved it. In fact, my values began to change. I would have liked to have had some youth (children) of my own. Just about that time, Good Pope John came on the scene. He believed in shared decision making and started to break the paternalistic approach of the church. He wanted things to be on an adult-to-adult level instead of a parent-child level. It looked as if everyone was going to have something to say in the Church. The whole atmosphere was changing. I belonged to a group of young priests who were working for change in the Church, and it looked as if married clergy were right around the corner. Then John died and Paul came in. Immediately it was clear. Paul seemed to have a different type of shared decision making than John. Paul made the decisions and shared the results. Hopes of a married clergy and shared decision making started to fade.

Taking a stand: a turning point

After a year of thinking it over, I resigned in 1968. I went to Colorado University for another degree in counseling and psychology. Actually, I was looking for someone to marry. My values had changed. I had done a lot of marriage counseling, and saw that it was easy to say "I do" but traumatic to say later "I don't". My main criteria was someone who liked children and someone who was flexible. I saw myself as free wheeling and not too organized, so I needed a flexible person for compatibility. I ended up with a "ringer"! I was just about ready to zero in on my number one choice when Fran came on the scene. She is flexible and she likes kids. We now have two "altar boys," Kevin and Kenny. I'm raising altar boys instead of training them.

The union card

After working as a high school counselor (which involved more paperwork than counseling), I was at the right place at the right time and got a grant to study for a doctorate or the "Union Card". To teach on the university level a person needs the "Union Card". The doctorate doesn't make you a good teacher, but you can't qualify without it.

Teaching teachers communication

After the doctorate program, I got a job teaching teachers how to communicate with children. This means how to enhance the self-concept of the children through communication. What a challenging job. People often ask why teachers need such a course since they are trained in the university to work with children. Actually, they are given a few courses in psychology. However, too many times the saying of a friend of mine is truer than its opposite: "Many of my psychology teachers were psychopaths who didn't have the decency to go crazy." Actually, that funny and exaggerated statement may come from the strong opinion that a number of people go into psychology to solve their own problems. Many go into psychology to learn tools to help others. Consequently, the caliber of psychology teachers will vary with their motivation for being in the field.

Communications Unlimited

After a year and a half of working for a school district, the increased demand for workshops in education and in the government made me seek a half-time contract in the school district. One person "in the know" said there would be no problem. Consequently, I got booked up for a lot of workshops. Finally, I put in my request. Surprisingly it was refused on the grounds that it would set a precedent. No one had ever gone from a full to a half-time contract in the history of the school district. I asked to talk to the school decision-making cabinet. They said that they wouldn't change. Fran and I decided that we had enough to make the house payments until May — then the sun shines — who needs a house? In February, 1974, I resigned and began "Communications Unlimited". At present it is four years old and, thank God, going strong.

Retired

I see myself as retired because I had planned to do communication workshops when I retired. The refusal of the half-time contract forced me into early retirement (15 years before my original retirement plan). My hobby is communication and it is a really neat feeling to make a living doing what I like best. I am still working part time as an off-campus instructor for the University of Northern Colorado teaching communication courses, e.g., "Enhancing Self Concept in the Classroom," and "Psychology of Communication in Marriage".

It has been a long, interesting ride from the stolen Capital Laundry truck to traveling in airplanes for Communications Unlimited. I've traveled the restricted roads of living up to others' expectations. Now I'm beginning to taste the wonderful experience of living up to my own expectations, and it is fun. I'm writing this book because I would like to share this experience with others. Having fun being yourself is an experience in love — and love has to be shared if it is to grow. To keep love, you have to give it away. In giving, you **Beat Stress and Live Longer**.

How did we get the title?

In October of 1977, I was teaching a university class in "Enhancing Self-Concept". I told them about this upcoming stress book and ran a title contest with prizes for Win, Place, and Show.

Marlene Summers had one, but told her friend, "It's not that good, so I'm not turning it in." Luckily, her friend convinced her to give it a try. Thanks to Marlene, whose creativity is much greater than she ever realized, her title won by a landslide, and this book was christened **B. S.* and Live Longer** (* Beat Stress).

You can't believe the stimulating reactions I have already received concerning the title. One fellow remarked, "Hell, just publish the cover and it will go."

Last Tuesday, I received a call from the trainer in the Veterans Administration in Fargo, North Dakota. He said, 'I'm looking for some stress-management workshops and I was referred to you. When I was told that you have a forthcoming book on stress entitled **B.S. and Live Longer**, I decided you are the guy for my workshops."

Frank McCarty, my accountant, firmly believes that B.S. in its original meaning is an essential ingredient of the art of living, as well as a stress reducer. With a twinkle in his Irish eyes, he said, "Now, B.S., my lad, is connected with the blarney stone. Take away B.S. and Ireland would not be the fun-loving place it is. B.S. embellishes a story, it makes it come alive, it adds personality. Don't confuse it with 'horseshit', which is intentional deceit with a sinister ulterior motive."

The more I thought about it, the more I realized how true it was. My thoughts swung back to my earlier years when I served my internship in B.S. under my brother Joe. He is gifted in B.S. I'd watch him tell stories that literally kept people in awe. They had as much enjoyment in the listening as he did in the telling. Neither party knew what was coming next. All went away happy.

B.S. in action

Not long ago, after working all morning, Dee and I decided to take a lunch break. We went to a nearby restaurant. We didn't find anything on the menu that turned us on. It's not fun to be in a place where you don't want to be, so we decided to try a combination of B.S. and assertiveness training. We decided to go to Duffy's instead, a famous fun place to eat. The waitress was due back in a minute with our coffee and to take our order.

In that time we created the following: "Ma'am, our watch stopped and we have to catch a plane. Our daughter is getting married in Las Vegas and it will be a disaster if we miss the wedding." The young waitress was so helpful. She gave us directions to the airport, was happy our daughter was getting married, and enthusiastically wished us a nice trip.

Instead of saying right out that we didn't like the menu and perhaps causing her stress, we added a touch of B.S. to the assertive recipe and she was happy. We had a delightful lunch at Duffy's, being where we wanted to be.

Frank was right. B.S. in its original form can reduce stress and add sparkle to your life.

Approach of this book

Six elements team up to give this book a unique flavor designed to make the message "come alive" in your life.

1. The receiving-giving-receiving approach

I have a lot of the child in me and maybe that is why I love to be with and talk with my two little boys. The other day I asked little Kenny, whose birthday was coming up, "If you had one wish, anything you wanted, what would your wish be?" He thought awhile, like a little philosopher, and then said, "Dad, I think I would like to have a K-Mart store. All I really want is the toy department. I could have all the toys I wanted. If I got the store, I would just take the toy department and give the rest to you." For Kenny, happiness is two things: having the toy department and giving the rest to dad. What a beautiful combination of not "giving and receiving", but "receiving and giving".

Kenny's philosophy is the basis for this book. I roam around the department stores of life in terms of the interesting people I meet in my seminars. They are from all walks of life . . . government people, teachers, secretaries, homemakers, business executives, single, married, divorced, etc. I meet people who think they are God (exaggerated self-image) and people who think they are nobody (low self-image). I meet loads of people in between. Since my hobby is getting inside their world to see how they perceive life, I receive abundant information and insight, and it livens up my life. Every day I learn something from someone that I can use in my "Me, Inc." whose goal it is to live a fulfilling life. Little Kenny receives a whole department store, but I receive a whole lot more . . . the intangible departments of peoples' lives. Kenny keeps the toy department, I keep the adult toys of insights, values, feelings and ideas that help me "have fun, not with toys, but by just being myself." Then I, like Kenny, give everything away . . . and it is a higher level of giving than material giving. I give away things that can help people live a fuller life, things that can arm them against the enemies of stress, and things that can help them find out who they are . . . and learn to like what they find.

There is an added element that is super neat and it gives me the "giving edge" over Kenny. He gives away the rest of the department store and it is no longer his. I give away immaterial insights and tools of living life to the fullest, but in giving them away, I still keep them for myself. In fact, in giving them away, they become more mine. It's like the old axiom, "You never learn until you have to teach." I'll add, "You never learn until you write." I've read volumes of stuff on stress. In writing it down so I could give it away, I really got a handle on it. This seems to fit the meaning of Christ's words, "In giving, you shall receive."

2. Talking-a-book approach

Talking and not writing is another facet of the approach in this book.

The fifty percent Irish in me gives a touch of blarney that the everyday person understands. So, I just sit here talking to you through my typewriter just as I talk to others through the microphone in my classes. Luckily I am totally stress-free when it comes to grammar, which doesn't box me in because I just "ain't got none", or is it "ain't got any?"

3. The real-life approach

Recently, someone in my marriage class took a previous course on "Marriage Communication" from a university professor who was not even married. I was not a bit surprised. I had an elementary counseling course from an instructor who had never set his foot in an elementary school. My university experience almost drowned me in theory overload. That is why I vowed not to teach anything in philosophy, psychology, or communication that I or others have not tried and found enriching for our everyday lives. In fact, one of the projects for my university class is, "write me a letter." The letter usually contains stories of how the teachers used the techniques of building self-image with their students or in their own lives. If you wonder where I get the quotes from all the letters, you now have your answer. In most cases I change the names, but all of the stories are real. This real life approach is especially vital in terms of coping with stress because it is literally a matter of life or death. If you don't learn how to deal effectively with stress, it will make you sick, age you prematurely, and sooner or later, kill you.

4. "You, Inc." approach

We would like you to approach this book as "You, Incorporated." You are in the business of attaining fulfillment in life. Stress used creatively can make your business prosper. Stress overload or "distress" will put you out of business. In these pages are many relevant tools to make your business of living life to the fullest become successful. Every "You, Inc." is a unique entity with various needs and aspirations. Take the things that can help you and leave the rest. It is the supermarket approach, taking what you want. If your business is stagnant, hopefully you can find something to bring it to life. If it is alive, hopefully you can find something to help it "live life to the fullest."

5. Non-stressful and non-profit atmosphere approach

Several years ago I was utterly frustrated in trying to find a book that would fit my seminars and classes. I tried everything. Nothing seemed to fit my style. I got rid of the helpless frustration by doing something about it. I sat down without knowing a "verb from a vegetable" and wrote **Having Fun Being Yourself**. I published it in 1974 through Communications Unlimited, my own consulting firm. It is now in its 5th printing and I've used the income from it to write **Re-entry Into the Single Life**.

Today I'm writing **B.S. and Live Longer**. In the next year or so, I will finish **Can Marriage Light Up All Your Tubes?**

Probably the most effective tool in coping with stress is to face it and do something about it. It really worked for me. From my frustration of not finding a book to fit my classes, I began writing. I'll probably never be a "Billy the Kid of England" (Shakespeare), but I now have a book company. All the money from book sales goes back into the book fund for future books. Beyond a doubt, it is the least stressful publishing company in America. There are no rules to box me in, no deadlines, no editor trying to translate it into English which he thinks is more appropriate. I really feel that I'm in touch with a lot of everyday people. I listen to them. I understand their hopes, fears, aspirations, and their problems. I talk a language which they can understand. In other words, I've got something to share based on what I've learned, and with my own book company, I can share it. And again, "in giving, I receive," so the non-profit book company is profitable because it gives me fulfillment, happiness, and a real sense of worth. Just one of the many letters saying, " . . . your book was a turning point in my life," is worth all the combined profit of the other big book companies. This book is written in a relaxed and stress-free atmosphere and I hope that in it you'll find a way to cope with stress so you can experience the real joy of relaxing and enjoying the precious gift of life by "Having Fun Being Yourself."

Of the people, by the people, and for the people

If there is anything that could summarize the approach of this book it is the Constitution of the United States. This book actually is "of the people" because the principal teacher is the lives of everyday people. This book is "by the people" because I have gathered together stories by different people all over America.

Actually, almost everyone who helped make this book a reality was a former participant in one of my classes. The cover designer, the title creator, the artist, the typist, and the letters and stories all came from people just like you. This book is "for the people" because it provides people with the tools to make "life, liberty, and the pursuit of happiness" a dream that can come true in their everyday lives.

A fun approach

When I was in the fourth grade, St. Leocretia (we called her Leo the Lion) said, "Jimmy, get that smile off your face, you are here to learn." In high school they told my parents, "Jimmy should be more serious." In college, when I floated a paper airplane in class, Mr. Van Ferik (a direct descendant of Hitler) said, "Mr. Keelan, you will play or learn . . . the door swings both ways, in or out." In the seminary, Father Moore (whom we called Moose) tried to take the fun part out of my life by saying, "A seminarian should take things more seriously." From kindergarten through college, if you smiled, they wondered what you were up to. Many classes were like a morgue with the professor as the funeral director. Some teachers had as many degrees as fahrenheit, but when it came to a sense of humor, they were like death eating a cracker.

Our culture has created a big parent and a little child in so many people. Seeing the humorous side of things is a magnificent stress reducer. Despite the somber and smileless tone of stress research and writings, I still think that you can learn much more if the creative child is allowed to liven up an adult-adult message.

It worked in football

For 17 years the Denver Broncos were a second-class football team. For 17 years Red Miller was an assistant coach. The 17-17 combination came together in 1977 and they ended up in the Superbowl. Many said Red Miller would never make a head coach because he was too much "one of the boys". He does not play the serious role of head coach. A major part of his philosophy is that you can "have fun and win at the same time."

One of his players summed it up well: "I learned to love football again under Red Miller. This is what I thought football should be. When I was in college, it wasn't fun, it was pressure. Now, even though football is my job, it is fun again." Red Miller has combined fun and winning, giving super job satisfaction and team spirit to his Cinderella team.

It works in class and seminars

For years I have tried to combine learning and fun in classroom settings and it has been rewarding. Research shows that the lower the anxiety level, the more the students learn. In my 22 years of schooling, I have had a number of teachers who created the atmosphere of death row. One professor held us accountable even for the footnotes. I got past all their tests, but I learned little. My real learning took place in those classes in which there was a relaxed atmosphere and the students were not in the parent-child role. I found through experience that you can smile and learn simultaneously.

It is at work in this book

As I said before, this book is made up from the lives of people. Among other things, people are funny. I had fun as well as deep satisfaction writing this book. Hopefully, this fun approach will help you get more out of this book so you can learn to **B.S. and Live Longer** . . . and fuller.

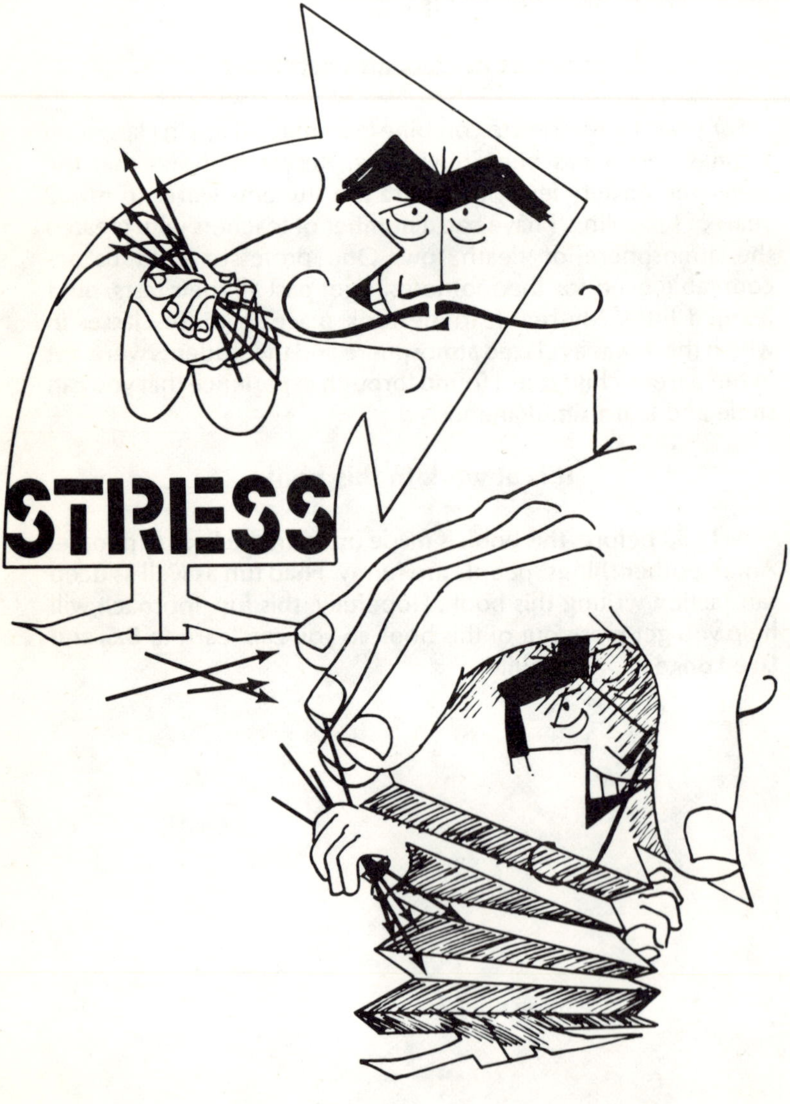
STRESS

CHAPTER 1

WHY IS STRESS THE NO. 1 KILLER IN AMERICA?

Americans want to be No. 1 in football, but if you have any smarts you won't try to be No. 1 in stress. As Dr. Hans Selye, a world authority on stress says, "It is a killer." Heart attacks are the No. 1 killer in the United States, and stress is almost always the culprit behind the heart attack.

Mental Illness

Go to a nearby neighborhood school yard and count out 25 children on the playground. Before they reach their lives' end, two will be hospitalized for the insane, four will become profoundly neurotic, four deeply neurotic, four mildly neurotic, and eight to ten will be fairly normal. What is the reason for these shocking statistics? "Repressed Stress." Many people adapt to repressed stress by going insane or becoming neurotic.

The President's Commission on Mental Health reports that between 20 million and 32 million Americans need mental health care. At any time, about 25% of the country is under emotional stress. A doctor might diagnose such people as suffering from depression or anxiety.

I remember from the days I was a priest in Hawaii my visit to a mental hospital where I was chaplain. I met a fellow in the hall and I said, "Good morning, I am Father Keelan." He said, "Nice to meet you. I am President Abraham Lincoln." I was taken aback. Nervously I asked, "Who told you you were President Lincoln?" He replied, "God did." Another man standing nearby yelled, "The hell I did!" Both men coped with stress, one thinking himself President Lincoln, the other God.

The vast results of stress are literally everywhere. Let's take a look at them.

1. Heart disease is the No. 1 killer, and stress is the No. 1 cause. In the United States, there are 1½ million heart attacks a year. One half of them are fatal.

2. Every year thousands of parents reduce their stress through child abuse.

3. Twenty million Americans have hypertension.

4. Researchers indicate that 3.3 million men reduce their stress by severely beating their wives. Surprisingly, Langley (co-

author of **Wife Beating**) reports that approximately one million husbands are beaten by their wives. He calls "husband beating" the most unreported crime in the nation, due to the fear of humiliation.

5. Students are reducing their stress in violence also. They are not only beating up one another, but assaults on teachers are on the increase. Stress bills run into the millions when they add up the destruction of school buildings and equipment caused by students letting out their stress through vandalism.

6. Millions of teenagers use running away from home as a stress outlet.

7. 124,000 Americans attempt suicide to try to eliminate their stress.

8. Another 24,000 succeed in suicide.

9. Several million Americans reduce their stress by becoming drug addicts.

10. America has millions and millions of workaholics who attempt to reduce stress through work; and most of them, unfortunately, don't even know that they are addicts. They hide their addiction under the virtuous and accepted cloak of the Protestant Work Ethic.

11. Valium (called "Pentagon popcorn" in the military) is the most widely purchased drug in America.

12. Ten to twenty million Americans reduce their stress by becoming alcoholics. One-third of the alcoholics are women, and some authorities believe the proportion closer to one-half. The real number is unknown because many (perhaps most) women alcoholics are "hidden". An added and often omitted feature is that they also increase stress for the bartender, as brought out by a poem my dad taught me.

> A man stood at the Pearly Gates,
> His face was pale and cold.
> He merely asked the man of fate
> Admission to the fold.
> "What have you done," St. Peter asked,
> "To seek admission here?"
> "I owned a tavern," said the man,
> "Sold whiskey, wine, and beer."
> The man turned nervously around;
> St. Peter touched the bell.
> "Come in," he said, "and have a drink,
> You've had enough of hell."

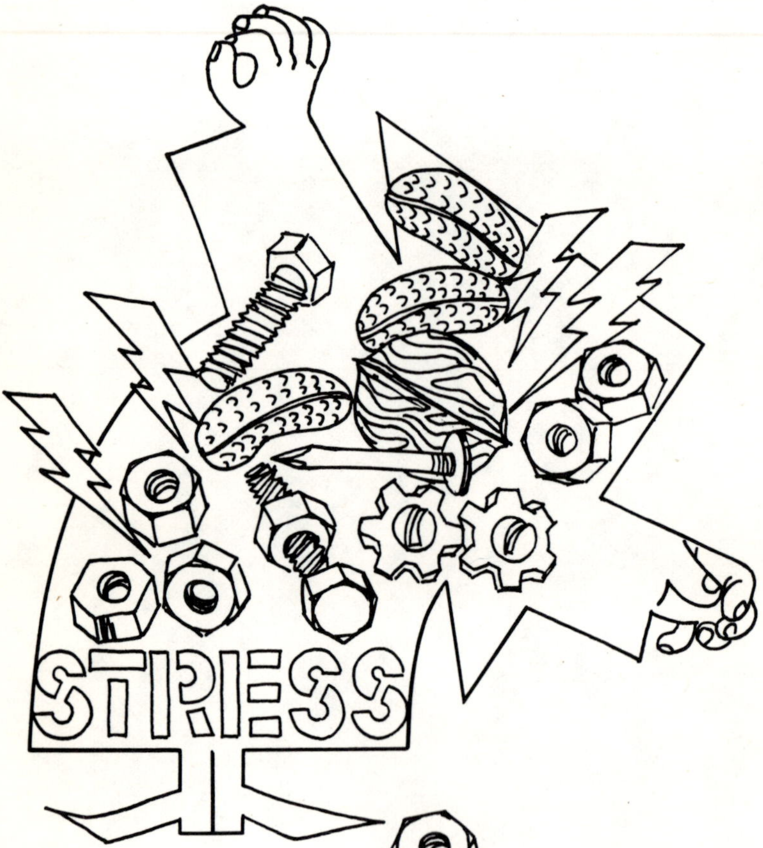
STRESS

CHAPTER II

WHAT ARE THE NUTS AND BOLTS OF STRESS?

First of all, stress is the response of the body to any demand made on it. It includes such warning signals as nervousness, sleeplessness, irritability, inability to concentrate, and the loss of muscle coordination.

Good stress

There is no way you can avoid stress, and "it ain't all bad". Good stress includes pleasant experiences of joy, fulfillment, self-expression, a passionate embrace or making love, the tension of normal expectations.

The impact of harmful stress

Dr. Selye pointedly shows the impact of harmful stress through an eye-opening experiment. He put 150 rats into a harness restraint so they could not move. Another 150 rats roamed free in their cages. All the rats were put on a high fat, high cholesterol and high sodium diet. The results couldn't have been clearer.

Every single one of the 150 restrained rats had a heart attack and died. Not one of the unrestrained rats had a heart attack.

For humans, this means that people under great stress run a radically higher risk of heart attacks.

In another dramatic experiment, Dr. Selye took two groups of 600 rats each and put them on a fast. One group had restraints put on. All 600 rats with restraints developed ulcers, all 600 without restraints remained ulcer-free. This indicates that it is not necessarily the food you eat that causes ulcers but the degree of stress you have.

For humans, this means that people under great stress run a radically higher risk of ulcers.

A limited inheritance of adapting power

Coping with stress takes energy. The human body goes through three stages when confronted with stress. This process is called the General Adaptation Syndrome. All higher organisms, human and animal, experience it when under stress. It is a two-edged sword which helps us to cope with danger but can hurt us after the danger passes.

These physical reactions are comparable to a military operation. Sentries sound the alarm when they see anything unusual. Soldiers move to standby, ready for combat. They need time to return to normal following the all clear. They will react less vigorously to a fresh alert. If they are kept constantly in a combat status they will eventually be unfit for battle.

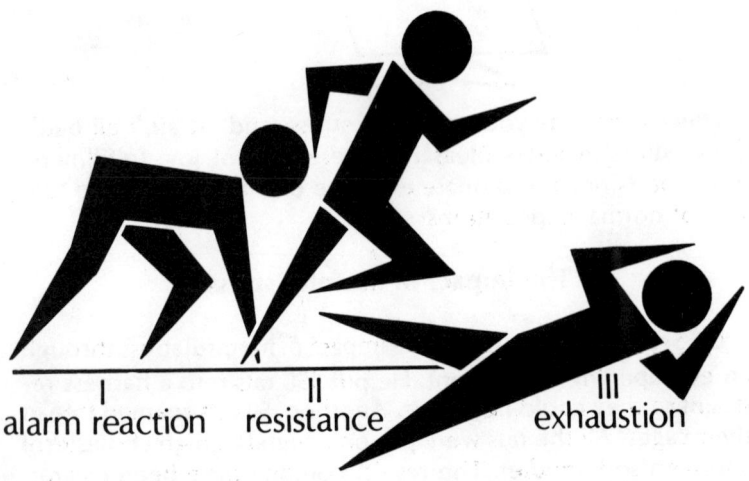

I alarm reaction II resistance III exhaustion

Likewise, our first bodily response to stress is an alarm reaction. It occurs when we first sense that something is out of the ordinary. The alarm reaction may be experienced suddenly as rage or fear, or it may be slow and more like a growing feeling of dread. Regardless of its speed of onset, it triggers adaptive actions within our bodies.

During the second stage, resistance, physical changes begin to prepare our bodies for action. Oxygen intake and pulse rate increase; the blood vessels constrict and increase the blood pressure; sugar and adrenalin flow into the blood stream. The total reaction provides us with extra energy and muscular tension to cope with danger. They continue until we use the built-up energy or neutralize the threat. They may continue until we enter the third stage, exhaustion.

Most stress reactions do not run to the point of exhaustion, but moderate resistance reactions may continue for such a long time as to cause serious damage, e.g. chronic anger can produce a constant excess of digestive juices . . . this produces ulcers by eating holes in the intestinal walls.

The principal point is that responding to stress takes energy. You can fight the stressor, you can flee from the stressor, or you can ignore, or tolerate the stressor, but they all take energy. Since man has a limited amount of adapting energy, it follows logically that the more the stress, the earlier the death. This vital response energy is like an inheritance . . . spend it carefully and it will last for years; squander it all in a short time and you will go bankrupt. Your "You, Inc." will be out of the business of living.

This book is designed to provide you with the essential tools needed to spend this inheritance carefully so that you can **Beat Stress and Live Longer.**

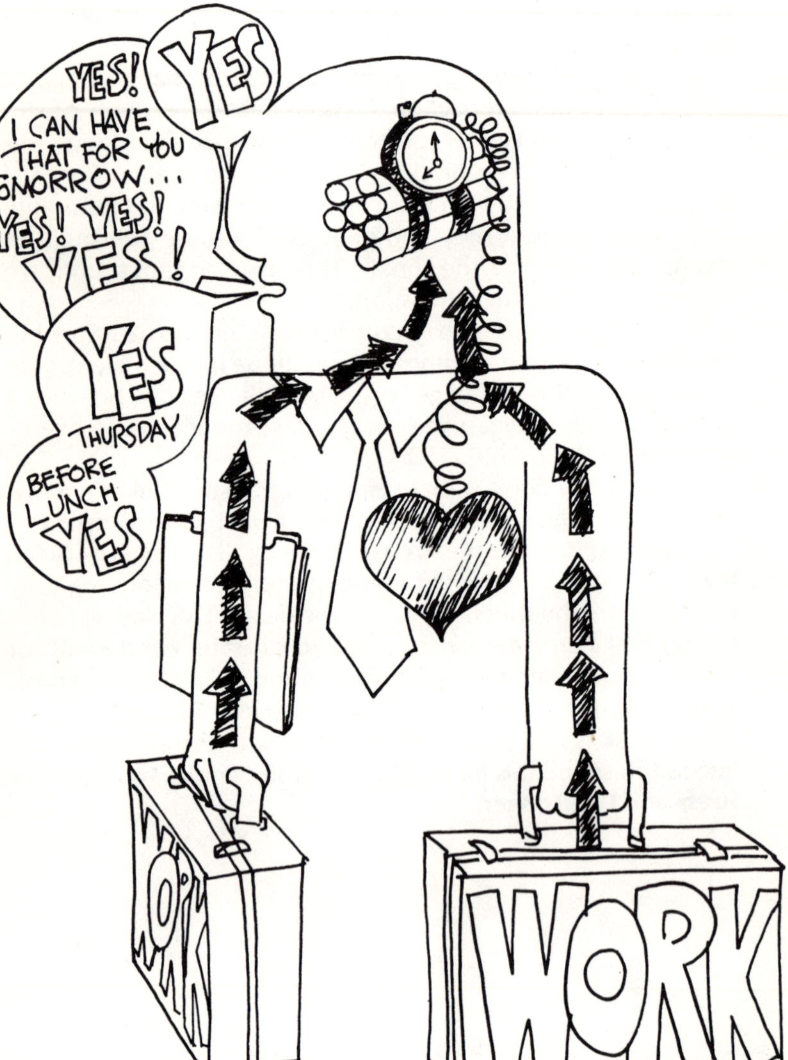
YES! I CAN HAVE THAT FOR YOU TOMORROW... YES! YES! YES!
YES
YES THURSDAY
BEFORE LUNCH YES
WORK
WORK

CHAPTER III

WHAT MAKES THE WORKAHOLIC TICK AND HIS HEART STOP?

During World War II all the able-bodied men were drafted. I was 16. Jobs were plentiful. My buddy, Tony, and I had a different job every week. If things didn't go our way we quit. Some called us lazy, others said we were the most likely not to succeed. I guess it was a little bit of both. We never were called workaholics (or even workers). Thank God, work never got the best of us then, and it never has since. In those days, the workaholic was the epitome of the "good person". Today things are slowly beginning to change. Researchers in the field of heart attacks are throwing a whole new slant on things. Now the workaholic is the person dependent on overwork for his "kicks" or "highs"... as is the speed freak on his amphetamines or the junkie on his heroin.

The "In" or "Out" group

The workaholic is an addict, but he or she doesn't know it and neither do the majority of people in America. They are still the "in group" and the other addicts are still the "out group".

Just sit back and analyze our culture and it will be more than clear. You've heard of the rewards for "Salesman of the Year," "Workman of the Month," etc. Have you ever seen a reward given by any company for "Alcoholic of the Year"? Visualize the company awards banquet. "On behalf of our company, I would like to present this plaque to Joe Rogers for 'Alcoholic of the Year'. He not only drinks at home, but he brings his philosophy of life to work with him . . . he drinks during coffee breaks, during lunch, and always carries a pint in his suit pocket, in case he has to cope with a stressful decision." Sounds ridiculous? Joe Rogers and the workaholic are both addicts. We reward one and look down upon the other. Discrimination?

Can you imagine a graduation awards ceremony where the principal is saying, "For the best grade point average, I am happy to give this award to Mike Kelsey, and for the best 'speed freak' the faculty has chosen Joe Smith. He was on grass for two years, but through courage, hard work and perserverance, he finally made the transition to 'speed'." Such awards ceremonies are unthinkable. Amazingly, the "salesman of the year" could be an addict. A workaholic is just as much an addict as the alcoholic is. The student receiving the high grade award could be a workaholic and just as much an addict as the "speed freak". The monumental difference is that society still rewards the workaholics by making them official members of the "in group", while the alcoholic or the drug addict is definitely in the "out group".

Stress research has created some new categories. The Type A person is like the car that is going full blast all the time. The Type A will get there first, but he or she will have a higher risk of an accident (heart attack). The Type B person is like a car that cruises. The Type B person won't get there as fast, but he or she will enjoy the trip along the way and have less chance of an accident. We all have characteristics of both. The art in living life to the fullest is to learn to acquire more of the philosophical type B behaviors and to keep your Type A tendencies from controlling your life. This is tough because society rewards Type A behaviors.

The woman of the year

Another example of society rewarding Type A behaviors was

given to me by Marge. She was talking about a friend of hers who had just won the "Woman of the Year" award in her home town. She showed me the write-up in the newspaper. Here is what I found about her Type A behavior.

1. She works relentlessly to make her home and yard beautiful. (Workaholic)
2. She keeps her house spic and span at all times. (Perfectionist)
3. She talks very fast, as if she has to get everything said in a hurry so she can get on to the next project. (Hurry sickness)
4. She never can say "NO". (Lack of assertiveness)

The whole article praised Type A behaviors. I said to Marge, "I don't know your friend, but I bet she can't 'relax and smell the roses'." Marge lit up, "You hit it on the head. You have to have advance notice to have a cup of coffee with her and then you feel you are on a time schedule."

This doesn't mean there should be no "Woman of the Year" awards. It really means we should expand the criteria to include the whole person and not just the "Worker of the Year".

My "A & B" classmates

A real life experience brings this into focus. I had two classmates in college, John and Vic. Vic was a workaholic. He studied night and day and always crammed for tests. He had all the Type A (workaholic) characteristics. He was nervous, uptight, always in a hurry, insecure, arrogant, and a poor listener.

He was one of the "in group" of the intellectuals. He got all the high mark honors.

John, on the other hand, was a philosophical Type B fellow. He didn't go to class to get A's. He went to see what he could learn to make his "You, Inc." more productive. He was a good listener, relaxed, easy to talk to. He never ran away with the high mark honors. Today John is in perfect health; alive, alert, fun loving, a good listener, and making some neat contributions to the world. In fact, he is the collaborator on this book.

Today Vic is recovering from bleeding ulcers, and last year had a 50-50 chance of surviving a major stomach operation. Vic was one of the "in group", but never learned the art of living.

How did "workaholics" become the "in group"?

Some wise old fellow once said that "we are products of our environment". I'll add to that, "If we want to change our lives, we have to question our environment and take a look at our past history." One quick look at history and we'll find out how workaholics were made the 'in group'.

1. Origin: Luther baptized work.

Before the Protestant Reformation, the idea of a vocation or calling applied only to the clergy who were separated from the rest of society. Luther bridged the separation by contending that laymen fulfill their Christian calling through their daily work. In essence, he said, "Work is just as much a Christian function as is praying in the monastery." This is the origin of the "Christian Work Ethic". Luther baptized work and brought it into the Christian fold.

2. Calvin made work the key to heaven.

Building on the ideas of Luther, John Calvin developed the basic outlines of the Puritan Ethic — now known as the "work ethic". He insisted that all work, no matter how humble, is a "calling" and worthy of its full reward in this world and the next. He went further when he said that, "The industrious, thrifty, honest Christian who is a good productive worker, becomes a member of the 'elect', predestined for eternal salvation." Talk about an awards banquet — a ring-side seat in heaven is the reward for hard work! To become successful and wealthy through hard work was a sign that you "made it" and became a "shoo-in", or predestined for heaven.

The Protestant Work Ethic was born from the joint ideas of

Luther and Calvin. It spread like wildfire among the working class. It gave comfort, hope and a bright future for all who had to work hard for a living.

A professor of theology (**Confessions of a Workaholic,** by Wayne Oates, p. 92) sums it up this way:

"A universal taboo is placed on idleness, and industriousness is considered a religious ideal; waste is a vice, frugality a virtue. Complacency and failure are outlawed, and ambition and success are taken as sure signs of God's favor. The universal sign of sin is poverty and the crowning sign of God's favor is wealth."

The by-product of the Christian work ethic: addicts

I hope that this history of the origins of workaholics doesn't give you the impression that work is bad. Like everything else, it is good in moderation. A drink or two in moderation is fine. Get addicted to alcohol and it is slavery. Work in moderation is fine, addiction to it is another form of slavery.

If you become a workaholic by way of the work ethic, your reward in heaven will be faster than anyone else's. You will get there quickly because workaholics are the ones who collect stress over-loads and are No. 1 in heart attacks.

How many workaholics are there?

Addictive behavior reinforces the concept of the work ethic and the American image of the successful executive is that of one who is aggressive and competitive. You'll find a number of managers that fall into this category. Friedman and Rosenman report that as many as 60% of all managers may fall into the category of workaholics, characterized by Type A behavior patterns (Type A Behavior and Your Heart, p. 202).

Type A behavior is not limited to managers. It is all over the place. For instance, while writing this book, we took breaks at a small coffee shop which was nearby. Here's what we learned. Doris, our regular waitress, had perforated ulcers. The other waitress had dangerously high blood pressure. The young cook could only sleep two hours a night and refused to see a physician. Type A behavior saturates the society. You may wonder just how much Type A you have in your own bloodstream.

Are you a Type A person?

We used to listen to "Jack Armstrong" when we were little. The story would always end in a life and death situation. Then the announcer would interrupt and say, "Tune in tomorrow to find out if Jack will survive his fight with the sinister frogman." Right now, you may be asking yourself the question, "Am I a workaholic, and if so, how can I change?" My answer is, "Keep tuned to this book. You'll be able to find out if you are a 50%, 75%, or a 100% thoroughbred Type A workaholic. Also you'll find the tools necessary to change your behavior, if you so desire."

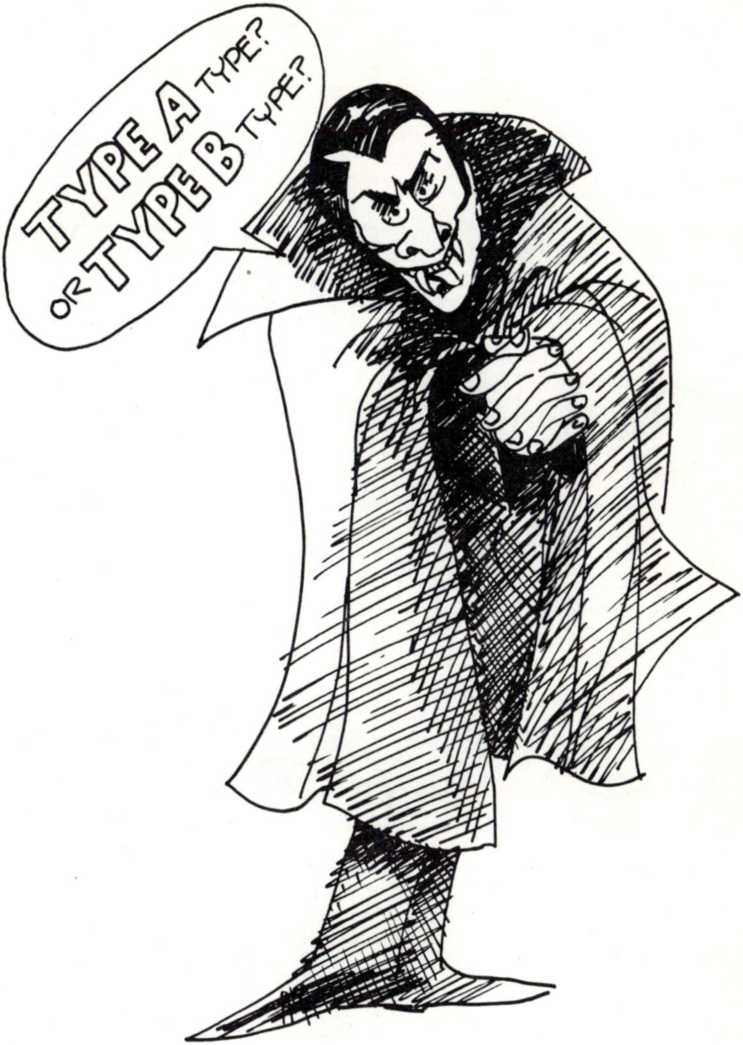
TYPE A TYPE?
OR TYPE B TYPE?

SHOULD OUGHT MUST vs. You, Inc.

CHAPTER IV

WHAT CAUSES STRESS IN THE EVERYDAY PERSON?

Somewhere, quietly sitting in the library at the university, is my doctoral dissertation. It was something I had to do to get a degree, a necessary ought. No one has ever read it. In fact, I wouldn't read it again myself. Actually, it turned me off on research. Now, five years later, I've learned to love research because it has meaning for me. I'm interested in keeping myself in good mental and physical health. I want to keep my "Me, Inc." a healthy, lively, fulfilling enterprise, and want to share my findings with the many other people who are also searching for happiness and fulfillment in life. Because stress is the No. 1 killer and has the power to put your "You, Inc." totally out of business with one fatal coronary, I've spent time tracking down this Enemy No. 1.

In fact, Annie Patrick, my colleague, and I got so interested in it that we decided to start doing some of our own research as well as reading what others have done. For several years, we have given a stress ranking sheet to hundreds of our workshop participants from all walks of life and from all parts of the country, including Hawaii.

Can you believe it — stress even in Hawaii?

Talk about stress reduction through doing something you like — I hated the work involved in my research for my dissertation. It was stress producing. I was fulfilling the "ought to" of my major advisor. On the contrary, I love the research we have done on stress because it is a "want to" as well as relevant to the real world. Anyway, here is what we found.

After all the research was in we found that job, spouse, children, and finances were the top four producers of stress. Sometimes the order varies, but they all were in the top four. One person who had finances as his No. 1 stress said, "I'll tell you why. When your outgo exceeds your income, then your upkeep becomes your downfall. That's been me ever since I committed matrimony 12 years ago."

Two differences

There were two major exceptions to the big four winning in every case. One exception came from the wives of Air Force officers (Majors on up). These military wives ranked social obligations as number four. The wives of the senior managers in the business world in Hawaii, however, outdid the military wives. They ranked social obligations as their No. 1 stress producer.

Can you sit back and analyze the reasons? You probably have the answer by now. You're right! It is because these obligations are real big "oughts". I've talked to these women. Often they have to invite people they don't like. They have to do a lot of false smiling and pretending they're happy. Several have said they are even restricted in what they wear. They have to wear something the boss will like. One woman said, "Jim did you ever hear of the song, 'I Sold My Soul to the Company Store'? Well, that's me."

Other women didn't consider social obligations a big stress. Why? They had a party or dinner when they wanted to. They invited whom they wanted to. Simply stated . . . if social activities are an "ought to" it takes the fun out of them and replaces the fun with stress. If they are a "want to" they become stress reducers instead of stress builders.

Philosophically, it goes back to that tremendous gift of free will. We feel good when we get to make choices. We feel stressful and frustrated when we have to do the things in which we have had little or no share in the decision. Stress is having little or no control over our life.

A seeming contradiction

We tallied the answers to the question, "What brings you the greatest satisfaction in life?" Guess what things appeared at the top? Spouse, children, job and money. The same things that cause stress in people also bring satisfaction. Of course, we do have the notable exceptions of those wives whose major cause of stress was social obligations. Naturally, social obligations did not rank as their major satisfiers. Social obligations in their case has only one side — pure stress.

Lisa's creative use of stress

A mother in one of my classes told me about the time her daughter used stress creatively. Lisa was a sophomore in college when she wrote the following letter:

Dear Mom and Dad,

Before you read this letter, please sit down in sturdy chairs. I didn't want to worry you so I didn't tell you about the fire in our dorm. The volunteer fire department was late in getting there so a young man in the filling station across the street got a ladder and saved me. Since I had no place to live, he was kind enough to let me share his apartment. We really had a nice platonic friendship going . . . but I guess the spirit is willing, and the flesh is weak.

Remember how you both looked forward to grandchildren . . . well, I think your wish is coming true . . . I am a little bit pregnant.

Michael is so nice, I can't wait until you meet him. He is an exchange student from Egypt but you won't mind, since you both are so liberal minded. Of course, Mom, you being a nurse, will not be frightened because I have a little case of V.D. I am sure it will disappear in no time.

I hope you are still in your chairs. Now take a deep breath and relax. There was no fire, no boy in the filling station. I am not pregnant and I don't have V.D. But I did flunk history. I'll be home in two weeks for vacation.

   Love,
   Lisa

Both parents jumped up and shouted, "Thank God!" How different their reaction would have been if she had come right out and said, "I flunked history." Her creative use of stress brought forth "Thank God" instead of "You are wasting our hard-earned money."

The lesson to be learned

Spouse, children, job, and money are the main satisfiers in our lives. They are also the principal causes of stress in our lives. The art of living lies in developing the satisfaction part of these big four stressors. This increases the assets of your "You, Inc.", and reduces the stressful elements, thereby decreasing the liabilities of your "You, Inc."

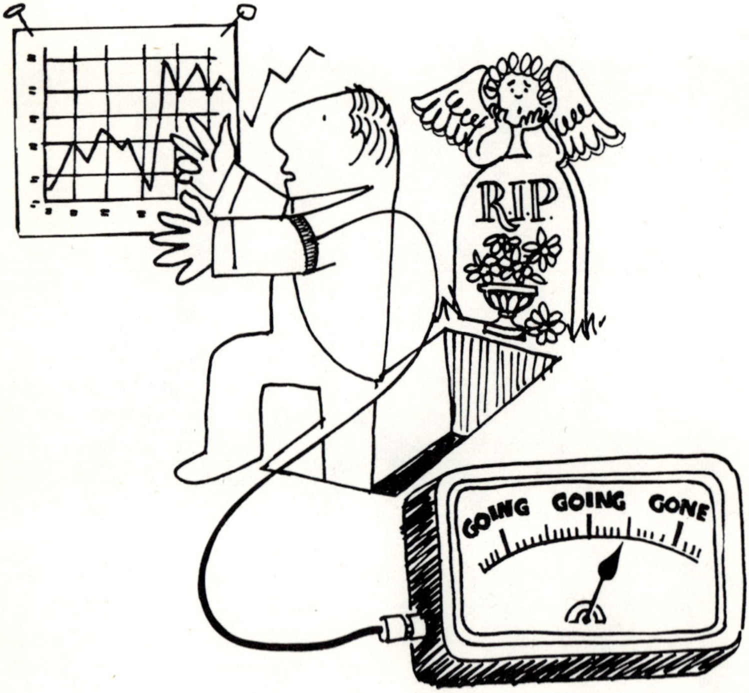
R.I.P.
GOING GOING GONE

CHAPTER V

HOW DO I SCORE ON THE STRESS ASSESSMENT TEST?

Last week Jan called to order some books. She said, "Did you know that Tom had a heart attack and open heart surgery? He has been off work recuperating for three months." She continued, "Remember last year when we attended your marriage workshop and we took the stress test? He scored over 500. At that time he ignored it. He was too busy to take the effort to reduce stress. Well, he has sure changed now, thank God. Twice a week a relaxation therapist comes over to tutor him on stress reduction techniques."

Tom is a typical Type A person if there ever was one. He is in his forties. Actually, since time is a high priority in his life he would have been three months ahead in time if he would have taken the preventative approach. When he scored high on the stress test, he should have pursued the stress reduction training at that time. Last week I visited Jan and Tom. He kept saying "I flunked your stress test."

This story brings out the purpose of this stress assessment tool. It is not a precision tool. It is, in my opinion, a marvelous preventative tool for both physical and mental health. In this case, "an ounce of prevention is worth many pounds of cure."

The interesting history behind the test

In 1930, Harold Wolff began studies of illness onset at Cornell University Medical College. In these pioneering years he found convincing evidence that common everyday events helped cause a host of diseases including many never previously considered "psychosomatic"; for example, colds, skin diseases and tuberculosis. One of the interesting things they uncovered was that visits by mothers-in-law were a major precipitant of common colds.

In a continuation of these studies, Dr. Holmes and other researchers interviewed many hundreds of tuberculosis patients between 1949 and 1964. In virtually every case examined they found that these patients had experienced increasing life change before becoming ill. Such events were financial problems, jail terms, marital separation, job changes, changes in residence, and personal injury. They began isolating specific life changes that repeatedly were a prelude to disease. Not all life events were negative. Vacations, personal achievements, births of children appear to also produce significant stress. Together with Dr. Rahe, a neuropsychiatric researcher with the Navy, Holmes asked thousands of men and women in every imaginable walk of life to judge and rank the impact of these events. From this data, they assigned numerical scores for each of the life change events. Then they tackled an enormous research project. They gave their stress tests (life, change, and scale) a trial run with thousands of people. This involved compiling their scores and following up to see if high scores had any health effects.

Holmes and Rahe were absolutely astonished at the results of their study, even intimidated by them... they didn't publish their findings for five years.

Since 1967 when they finally released the Life Change Scale (which I call the Stress Test, because it attempts to measure the degrees of stress involved with life events) it has been retested with thousands of subjects in the U.S., Japan, France, and all over the globe. The results are the same. TOO MUCH CHANGE OVER A SHORT PERIOD OF TIME INITIATES ILLNESS, AND THE GREATER AMOUNT OF LIFE CHANGE, THE MORE SERIOUS THE ILLNESS.

How does it work?

To take the test, check any of the events listed that have occurred in your life in the past 12 months. Your total score measures the amount of stress you have been subjected to in the one-year period and can be used to predict your chances of suffering serious illness within the next two years.

For example, a total score less than 150, means you have only a 35 percent chance of becoming ill in the designated period. If your score is between 150 and 300, you have a 51 percent chance of suffering poor health. If your score is more than 300, you are

facing odds of 80 percent that you will become sick — and as the score increases, so do the odds that the problem will be serious. We caution you, however, to remember that a high score is **not** a guarantee of illness, it is simply an indication, according to Dr. Holmes, that because of the stress you have been subjected to, there is a chance of becoming ill.

You are now ready to take the stress test (Adapted from T. H. Holmes and R. H. Rahe, "The Social Readjustment Rating Scale," **Journal of Psychosomatic Research**, 11, 1967, pp. 213-218).

The Social Readjustment Rating Scale
(Life Change Scale)

Life Event	Mean Value
1. Death of spouse	100
2. Divorce	73
3. Marital separation	65
4. Jail term	63
5. Death of close family member	63
6. Personal injury or illness	53
7. Marriage	50
8. Fired at work	47
9. Marital reconciliation	45
10. Retirement	45
11. Change in health of family member	44
12. Pregnancy	40
13. Sex difficulties	39
14. Gain of new family member (a birth, adoption, oldster moving in)	39
15. Business readjustment (e.g., merger, reorganization, bankruptcy)	39
16. Change in financial state (a lot worse off or a lot better off than usual)	38
17. Death of a close friend	37
18. Change to different line of work	36
19. Change in number of arguments with spouse (either a lot more or a lot less than usual regarding child rearing, personal habits)	35
20. Mortgage over $10,000 (e.g., purchasing a home, business)	31

21.	Foreclosure of mortgage or loan	30
22.	Change in responsibilities at work (promotion, demotion, lateral transfer)	29
23.	Son or daughter leaving home (e.g., marriage, attending college)	29
24.	Trouble with in-laws	29
25.	Outstanding personal achievement	28
26.	Wife begin or stop work	26
27.	Begin or end school	26
28.	Change in living conditions (e.g., building a new house, remodeling, deterioration of home or neighborhood)	25
29.	Revision of personal habits (dress, manners, associations, etc.)	24
30.	Trouble with boss	23
31.	Change in work hours or conditions	20
32.	Change in residence	20
33.	Change in schools	20
34.	Change in recreation	19
35.	Change in church activities	19
36.	Change in social activities (e.g., clubs, dancing, movies, visiting)	18
37.	Mortgage or loan less than $10,000 (e.g., purchasing a car, TV, freezer)	17
38.	Change in sleeping habits (a lot more or a lot less sleep, or change in part of day when asleep)	16
39.	Change in number of family get-togethers	15
40.	Change in eating habits (a lot more or a lot less food intake, or very difficult meal hours or surroundings)	15
41.	Vacation	13
42.	Christmas	12
43.	Minor violations of the law (e.g., traffic ticket, jaywalking, disturbing the peace)	11

Are you a high scorer?

Life is funny. We usually like high scores . . . a sign of excellence. In this case a high score is perhaps a sign that you may be walking on the edge of an avalanche and going through a highly stressful period of your life. Remember, a real high score (450 and above) means that you have a 90% chance of getting seriously sick. You can also go with the 10% chance that you won't and take a gamble. If you do go with the 90% chance, you may want to sit back, look at your life, and decide to do something to reduce stress in your life. Even if you didn't score high in the stress test, you still may want your stress at a lower level.

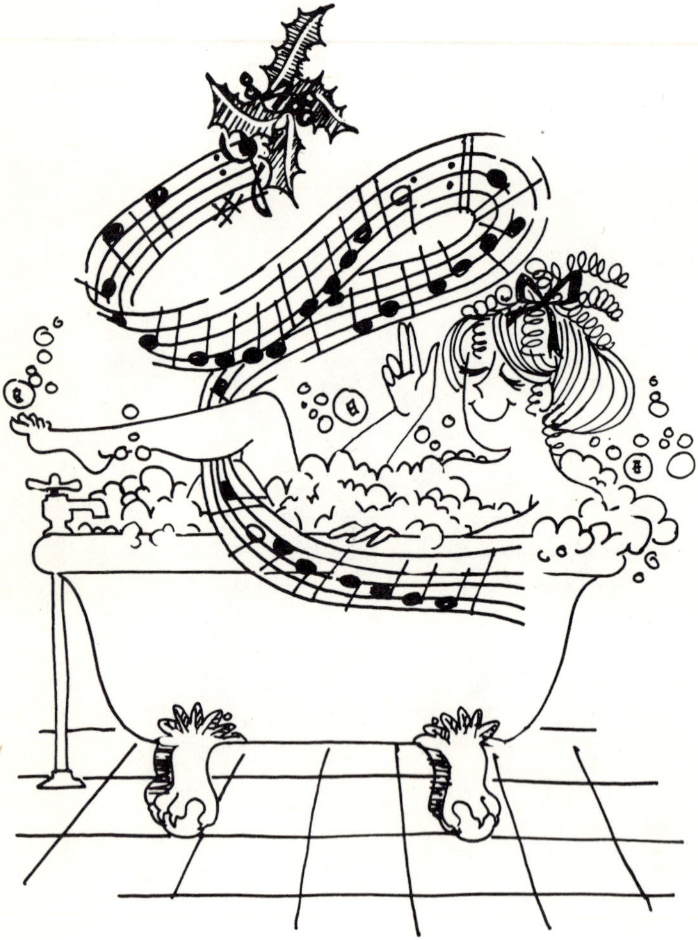

CHAPTER VI

HOW THE EVERYDAY PERSON REDUCES STRESS

In our research on stressors, we asked the question, "What do you do to reduce stress in your life?" The answers have become a stress reducing aisle in our supermarket. You can look them over and choose whatever may help your "You, Inc." reduce the liability of stress.

1. I watch T.V.
2. I shoot pool when I get uptight.
3. I get a baby sitter and take a night off.
4. I take a bubble bath and play Christmas records even in the middle of summer.
5. I paint a picture. I'm an artist and it really reduces stress.
6. I drink Johnnie Walker and listen to Frank Sinatra records.
7. I quit smoking and it has done wonders.
8. I talk to my dog every day for an hour.
9. I get a piece of paper and write out all my feelings.
10. I reduced stress by changing diets from meat to fish and fowl and no junk food.
11. I listen to others and get into their world and forget all about my problems.
12. I go on a shopping splurge.
13. I play the piano. It does wonders.
14. I talk to my best friend.
15. I get a bottle of wine, go to skid row and treat two bums and myself to a wine and cheese party. After listening to their stories, my stress pales into insignificance.
16. I finally got addicted to jogging. I meditate when I jog. What a combination! It has reduced a lot of stress in my life.
17. I eat. That isn't the best way, but that's what I do. I can measure my stress level by seeing how much weight I gain.
18. I go to an X-rated movie.
19. I get away from people and think and talk to myself.
20. I pound on the bean bag.
21. I go out in a field and scream as loud as I can. If I'm driving, I roll up the windows, turn the radio up, and shout as loud as I can. It works wonders.
22. I sew. It is my hobby.
23. I clean the house at full speed. It looks like a palace.

24. I work in the yard. I used to play golf, but I get mad and break clubs. It increased my stress. I'm a Type A and too damned competitive.
25. I drink scotch and play the record, "Make the World Go Away".
26. I got cheated in a used car deal. For months I diverted my stress into getting my money back. I finally did.
27. I went through bio-feedback therapy and learned how to relax.
28. I do transcendental meditation.
29. I try self-hypnosis.
30. I go to sleep.

Face it or flee

We reduced the research to the above 30, which is rather representative. There are a few unusual methods. What did we learn from this research?

The two ways humans react to stress is "flight or fight" which I call "face it or withdraw". Most people withdraw. Undoubtedly, we should use these reduction techniques, but when possible we should find the cause and deal with the stress at its source.

The band-aid approach

When you use the stress reduction methods without checking

what generates stress in your life, you really are taking the band-aid approach. You find them advocated as the solutions in a lot of stress writings. This approach doesn't get to the heart of the matter and is risky because a stress generator may produce more stress than you could handle through reduction methods.

The story of Al

Al taught in an extremely stressful high school. The stress was caused by a principal who felt he helped God with the creation of the world. Al got his stress out by jogging two miles a day. Unfortunately, his job generated more stress than he could get rid of by jogging. He died of a heart attack at school on the way to a class. He was 41 years old.

The story of Marge

I know Marge well. She copes with a lot of stress because the only decision she made in her marriage was 17 years ago when she said, "I do". After that Ralph took over. For six months she was in Transcendental Meditation. Research has indicated that it is an effective stress reducer. In her case, it could not reduce it as fast as the relational parent-child marriage could produce it. She ended up with a serious coronary. She did survive and is still recovering.

The moral of these stories

These are true stories and there are many more like them. The lesson in these stories is that you may be much better off if you identify the generator of stress and try to shut it down. At the same time make use of the stress reduction techniques.

I realize in some cases, you may feel you are boxed in and can't do anything about the generator. I happen to believe that when your adult is chairman of the board in your "You, Inc.", you can do something. It could be to plan for the day when you can shut down the generator. Planning, at least, reduces the helpless feeling that is an added stress.

It takes more energy to face it

To face the generator and do something about it initially takes more energy and causes more stress. Over a long haul you save loads of stress. Nowhere is this more true than in the field of re-entry into the single life. It takes a lot of energy and causes a lot of stress to accept the fact that a marriage is dead. It is a lot more stressful to attempt to live a relationship that has died. It is like going steady with a corpse.

This brings us to perhaps the most important chapter in this book: WHAT ARE YOUR STRESS GENERATORS?

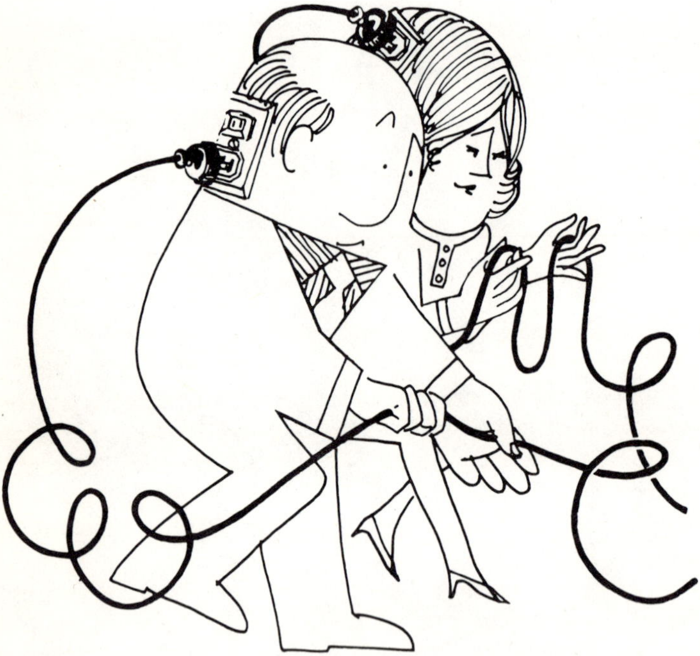

CHAPTER VII

WHAT ARE YOUR STRESS GENERATORS?

Do you, like most, use the band-aid approach to stress? Reducers deal only with the symptoms, not the causes. Jogging will reduce stress. Pinpointing the generators of stress in your life and coping with them will bring you peace of mind by reducing stress at its source.

In this chapter, we hit at the very core of the question. We have identified some major generators of stress. Now it is your turn. You have to ask, "Does this generator apply in my life?" If it does, what can you do to shut it down or at least significantly reduce its generating power? The length of this chapter signifies its extreme importance for effectively beating stress.

1. Do I have a philosophical generator?

Now don't let the word philosophy throw you. It comes from the words — love and wisdom, meaning love of wisdom. Wisdom combines theory and application. The love of wisdom is not the theoretical ivory tower and not the Type A do, do, do. Wisdom is the combination of the search for truth with the constant application to daily life to make life more meaningful and fulfilling.

You don't have to have a bunch of degrees to be a philosopher. One way to understand the values which make people tick is to listen to what they say. "My daughter got straight A's." "My son had perfect attendance." "Joey is a real go-getter. He's got drive." In no time we can see that DOING is a major component of the American philosophy.

Listen more closely and you'll find the purpose of all the doing. "My son just bought a $100,000 home." "We thought it would be nice to have a mountain condominium." "Our son-in-law, would you believe, has three degrees." "We felt that we just had to have a swimming pool." "My boyfriend has a Mark IV."

Put two and two together and you have another major element of the American philosophy, HAVE. Do, do, do, in order to have,

have, have. Now sit back and recall how many times you have heard, "I like Joe, he is so free to be himself."

Why is it so rare to hear a statement like that? Because "Being" is not a major value in the ordinary American's philosophy. In terms of "win, place, and show" the American philosphy is "Doing, Having, Being" as illustrated in the drawing below.

It is society-wide

The hippie movement to a great extent was a revolt against this philosophy. They were trying to say that there is more to living than two cars, money, and a nice house in the suburbs. They made people reassess, but the "Doing, Having, Being" philosophy is still the major force. In schools, the National Honor Society goes to those with the best grades... the doers. Have you ever heard something like this at awards night, "This award goes to Mike Jones because he has developed the talent of being himself." Now, being yourself is probably one of the greatest talents as well as the most challenging goals in life, but it is not rewarded by our educational society. That is why our kids come out of our schools with the "Doing, Having, Being" philosophy.

The thrust of religion, in terms of the Protestant Work Ethic, rewards the same philosophy. It also holds out an eternal reward to the successful doers that have "made it" as we discussed in the history of the Protestant Work Ethic.

Why does "Doing, Having, Being" produce stress?

There are a number of reasons why this philosophy of life produces stress.

1. Basically, it is a philosophical disaster. It is this very nature of man to know who he is. It is chaotic to be running around like a souped-up hot rod going full blast without any sense of direction.

2. Most Americans don't know themselves and that creates stress. Recently I had a drink with a successful "doer" with an ulcer. He was having marriage problems. He said, "My dad wanted me to make something of myself. I did. I went to college and received a Masters in business. I have a big job, pull down $55,000 a year, but I'm empty inside. I'm really beginning to question who I am and what I want to do with my life."

3. We should be loved and accepted for being, instead of doing or having. How often have you heard, "That is a good boy, you got all A's?" "I see that you'll never fill your brother's shoes, he was a go-getter." We quickly learn the rules of the game. If we want love and acceptance, we had better produce. The stress producing factor is a big one. We are often not loved for who we are as persons, but for what we produce. Our product-oriented society, instead of a person-oriented society, is a major generator of stress. Why do so many people fold up and die within three years after retirement? Simply because they feel that they are no longer productive, they lose their worth because their worth was dependent on doing.

4. This philosophy literally mass produces the Type A personalities who are definitely No. 1 in terms of heart attacks. They lead the league.

Are you a Type A person?

To bring this "Doing, Having, Being" philosophy right into the living room of your home (so you can check out to what degree it is a stress generator in your life) we have the Type A personality test (Adapted from "Type A Behavior and Your Heart").

Type A Personality Test

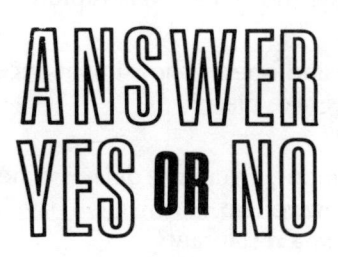

ANSWER YES OR NO

1. Do you have a habit of explosively accentuating key words in your ordinary speech . . . and finishing your sentences in a burst of speed?

Yes ☐   No ☐

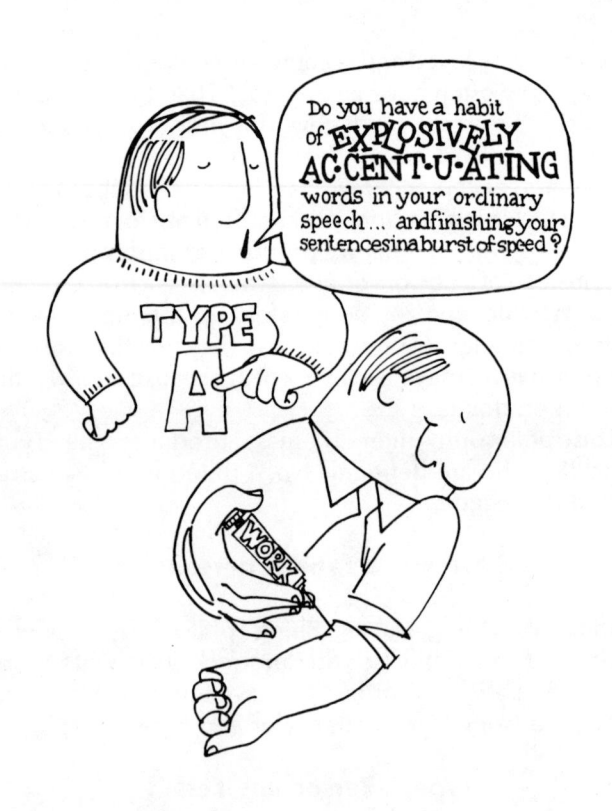

Do you have a habit of **EX·PLO·SIVE·LY AC·CENT·U·A·TING** *words in your ordinary speech ... and finishing your sentences in a burst of speed?*

TYPE A

2. Do you always move, eat, walk rapidly?

Yes ☐   No ☐

3. Do you feel and openly show impatience with the rate at which most events take place?

Yes ☐   No ☐

4. Do you get unduly irritated at delay — when the car in front of you seems to slow you up — when you have to wait in line, or wait to be seated in a restaurant?

Yes ☐   No ☐

5. Does it bother you to watch someone else perform a task you know you can do faster?

Yes ☐   No ☐

6. Do you often try to do two things at once (dictate while driving or read business papers while you eat?

Yes ☐   No ☐

7. Do you almost always feel vaguely guilty when you relax and do absolutely nothing for several days (even several hours)?

Yes ☐   No ☐

8. Do you not have any time to spare to experience being because you are so preoccupied with having?

Yes ☐   No ☐

9. Do you attempt to schedule more and more in less and less time without allowing for unforeseen contingencies (chronic sense of time urgency)?

Yes ☐   No ☐

If most of your answers were "no", you are a Type B. If you answered most of them "yes", you may be a Type A personality. If you think you are, you may want to check out further some of the characteristics of the Type A personality.

1. Poor listener — usually preoccupied
2. No real philosophy of life
3. Heavy smoker and coffee drinker
4. Uses cocktails at lunch, dinner, and in the evening to relax
5. No regular exercise pattern
6. Tense, aggressive, and often depressed when things don't go his way
7. Acting superior but feeling inferior inside
8. Lonely
9. Gets a sense of worth from amount of work accomplished
10. Hidden fear of others
11. Acquaintances, but few if any real friends

Type A and Type B in real life

Looking at the same thing in different ways is helpful to get a clearer picture. John Garquhar, director of Stanford's Heart Disease Prevention Program, documented it well in an article "Stress and How to Cope With It". I have adapted it to fit the lives of Peter and Ben.

A comparative study of two executives, Ben, a Type B, and Peter, a Type A, really would make anyone sit up and take notice. Both men are in their early fifties. In the next ten years, Peter, a thoroughbred Type A, will have a 95% chance of a heart attack. Ben, a Type B, on the other hand, will have a 5% chance of a heart attack in the next twenty years.

PETER
TYPE A

BEN
TYPE B

Potential Stresses	(Stressed, ineffective responses)	(Relaxed, effective responses)
1. 7:00 a.m. Alarm clock did not go off. Overslept. Awoke at 7:30.	**ACTION** Rushed through shaving, dressing, and breakfast.	**ACTION** Called colleague to say he would be 30 minutes late. Calmly got dressed and ate breakfast.
	THOUGHTS I can't be late. This is going to foul up my whole day.	**THOUGHTS** This is not a big problem. I can manage to make up the 30 minutes later on.
	RESULTS Left home in a hurried state.	**RESULTS** Left home in a calm state.
2. 8:00 a.m. Traffic jam caused by slow driver in fast lane.	**ACTION** Honked horn, gripped steering wheel hard; tried to pass and later tried to speed.	**ACTION** Waited for traffic jam to end. Relaxed while waiting; later drove at his normal rate.
	THOUGHTS Why can't that jerk move into the slow lane. This infuriates me.	**THOUGHTS** I'm not going to let this upset me, since there is nothing I can do about it.
	RESULTS Blood pressure and pulse rate rose. Arrived at work hurried and harried.	**RESULTS** Remained calm and relaxed. Arrived at work fresh and alert.
3. 10:00 a.m. Angry associate blows up over a staffing problem.	**ACTION** Is officially polite but nonverbal behavior signals impatience and anger.	**ACTION** Listens attentively; relaxes while listening carefully and mentally rehearses how he will handle this encounter. Is calm in demeanor.
	THOUGHTS This guy is a prima donna. I can't tolerate outbursts like these; I'll never get my work done.	**THOUGHTS** Beneath all his anger he does have a point. I can take care of this problem now before it gets more serious.
	RESULTS Associate storms out unsatisfied. Mr. A is too aggravated to take care of important business on his agenda.	**RESULTS** Associate's temper is calmed. He thanks Mr. B for hearing him out. Mr. B is glad that he was able to alleviate a potential problem situation.
4. 12:00 noon. Behind schedule.	**ACTION** Ate lunch in office while working. Could not find materials in files. Telephone calls made but parties were out.	**ACTION** Went for 20-minute walk in park. Ate lunch in park.
	THOUGHTS I'll never get out from under all this work. I'm going to plow through this if it takes all night.	**THOUGHTS** A break in routine refreshes me. I work better when I allow myself intervals to relax.

5. 10:30 p.m. Bedtime.	RESULTS Mistakes made in work because of exasperation. ACTION Insomnia for two hours. THOUGHTS Why don't I accomplish more? I am a disappointment to myself and my family. RESULTS Awoke exhausted and depressed.	RESULTS Returned refreshed. Proceeded with work rapidly and with insight. ACTION Fell asleep rapidly. THOUGHTS It's been a good day. I was able to handle several potential problems in an effective manner. RESULTS Awoke refreshed and happy.

I often jokingly open up a stress workshop with a "B.S." research study. In a serious voice I say, "I know most of you are aware of the Harvard study on stress. It has proven beyond reasonable doubt that just one coronary attack that is fatal will significantly reduce effectiveness at work." They all laugh (except the few who missed the joke). The strange thing is that a lot of people would be alive today if they realized the impact of that statement. Heart attacks are still the number one killer. Somewhere in the past someone summed it all up so well when he or she wrote, "Death is just nature's way of telling us to slow down."

"Hell, I'm lucky to be a Type B"

Two weeks ago, Ed had a birthday party. He was 43. While discussing **B.S. and Live Longer**, including Type A and B, he suddenly broke out in a beaming smile and said, "Well, I'll be damned. My parents and teachers always thought I was 'asleep at the switch' because I wasn't a high achiever like my Type A sister. Hell, after talking to you, I feel lucky. I'm a Type B."

Type A's and workaholics

A Type B is an effective worker, but will never become a workaholic. Type A's can and often do. Read carefully the following research on Type A managers taken from "Coping With Stress and Addictive Work Behavior" by Suojanen and Hudson. "It is our contention that 'distress' type situations in organizations frequently are the result of compulsive or addictive behavior on the part of managers. We further contend that much of such dysfunctional behavior on the part of managers is the result of their attempts, unknowingly, to satisfy their needs for a 'high' from work or crisis management, which is physiologically exactly the same as that sought by the alcoholics and the drug addicts. The workaholics are just as dependent on the 'high' they get from earning their daily bread as the 'speed freaks' are on their pills. The only difference is that the drug abusers seek 'better things for better living through biochemistry' by popping pills, whereas the workaholics create their chemicals in their own minds." Due to the Protestant Work Ethic our culture still rewards workaholism as a virtue. Until we have a cultural change, Type A will still abound.

The solution

"The Great Books" had the right idea. Take a look at the great thinkers of all time, that is, the philosophers. The philosopher, by nature, is a Type B. Included here is their perception, which is in line with the very nature of man.

Notice some significant points.

1. Being oneself is the base. Since "know thyself" is a goal that you can't fully reach, you are on a continual growing curve.

2. Then, you choose to do the things that fit you as a unique person and in essence you begin to "Have Fun Being Yourself." You get real fulfillment through your work activity because it is an actual expression of yourself and not the fulfillment of the oughts and expectations of others.

Talk about stress reduction, the leading expert in stress, Hans Selye, contends that doing what you want to do is one of the greatest stress reducers.

3. At last comes "Having" which is determined by what you need and not by what the Jones have. The result of the philosophical or Type B approach is significant:

A) Control of distress through clear basic values;

B) Use of stress creatively by doing what fits you as a person;

C) Peace of mind because you have a solid foundation and philosophy of life that will not topple in the face of the winds and storms of life.

HOW do you acquire this philosophical approach?

1. "Man is a product of his environment" doesn't have to apply to you. You can live in our "do-oriented" society and be a "being yourself" oriented person.

2. All you have to do is make the philosopher's system your own. It may take re-thinking, meditation, questioning and practice to put the "I CAN" attitude into being but you'll be living life to the fullest.

3. Live Life One Day At A Time — This is a basic rule of Alcoholics Anonymous. It works wonders for them. It'll work for workaholics also. Taking it one game at a time, Red Miller, the new Denver Bronco head coach, led the underdog Broncos to the A.F.C. championship in one year. It works in sports. It works with alcoholics. It will work for you.

Coping with stress with "Being, Doing, Having" philosophy

A letter from Mary explains.

Dear Jim,

Your course came at an ideal time. This "being, doing, having" approach really brought peace of mind. As you know, my boss is in charge of training. He hasn't done anything in the last four years. Well, he just got an advancement to a GS-13 (Government advancements run from 1-18). I was refused my 10. I, of course, organize all the training in the agency, and he takes the credit. I could take a transfer to another agency, but once I saw that both my GS-10 and his GS-13 are **"having"** *goals and training for me is "doing" what fulfills me, I can take a boss who literally does nothing.*

> *Sincerely,*
> *Mary*

Mary has peace of mind because instead of the Type A "Doing, Having, Being" philosophy, she has the "Being, Doing, Having" philosophy, or Type B.

A personal example of this philosophy shows that it can decrease the stress liability in your "You, Inc." and increase your assets of personal serenity. It is challenging to apply it to your life. Four years ago I had to move due to a job change. Our boys were almost ready for school so, "Being" was No. 1. In this case their "Being Happy" determined where we would move. We researched the area, found the best school (Being) and then bought the house (Having). It paid off so beautifully. Fortunately, I knew the principal, Jim Crammer. He loves children. Every day we see our two little blond boys happily running to the bus stop to go to Stott Elementary School. There the principal and staff create a warm and accepting atmosphere and give the kids the basics with lots of tender loving care.

2. Do I have a psychological stress generator?

As we mentioned in the beginning, you are in the business of living a fulfilling life as "YOU, INCORPORATED". You have time and life — two vital resources. The goal of your corporation is trying to live a happy, fulfilled life.

The greatest internal obstacle in your corporation is the parent.

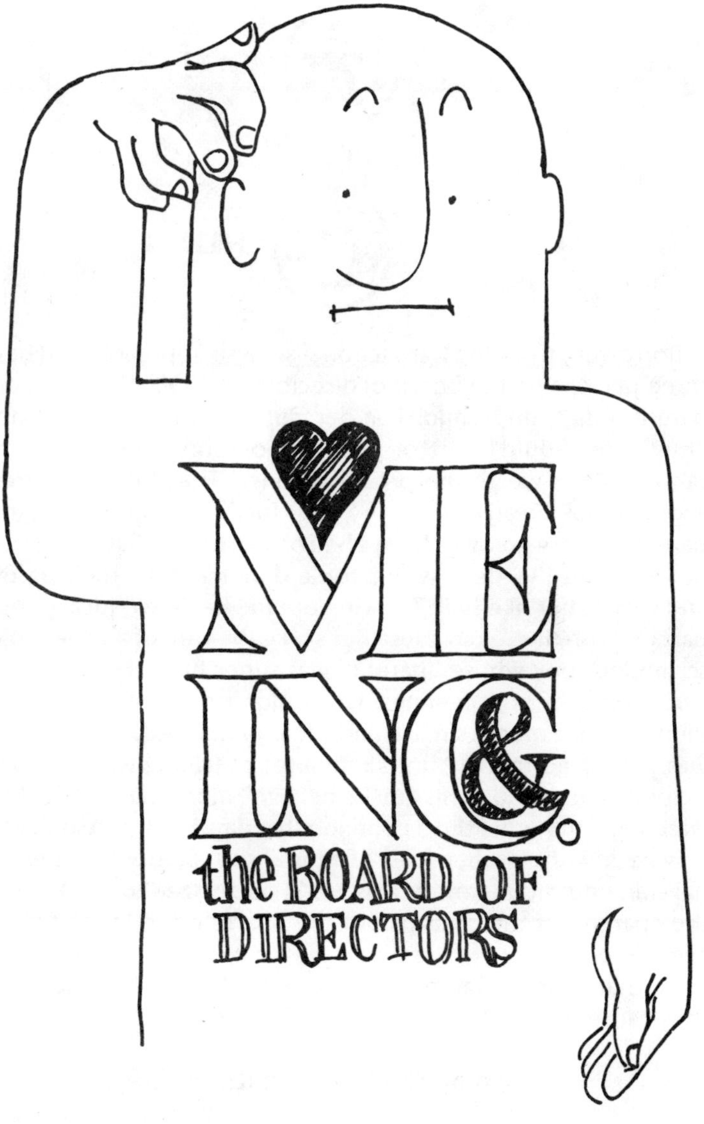
ME INC&.
the BOARD OF DIRECTORS

PARENT

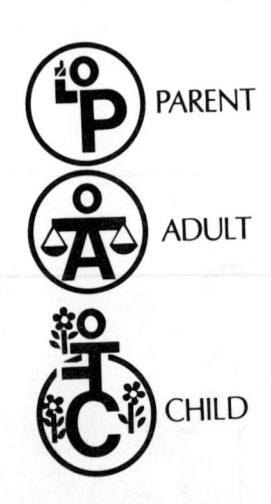

ADULT

CHILD

Borrowing from the transactional analysis approach, you have three persons on the board of directors of "YOU, INC." — your parent, adult, and child. For our purposes, the parent is the "ought or should" part of your corporation. The adult is the rational "let's weigh the pros and cons." The child is the free, spontaneous creative part. If "You, Inc." is controlled by the parent, you are going to have a hell of a lot of internal stress. I use hell because I've dealt with people dominated by their parent and they suffer like hell. To bring out the hell the critical parent part of "You, Inc." can cause, let's take the case of a 13 year old, scrupulous boy whose "parent" was super huge. He had semi-truck loads of guilt feelings. He couldn't do anything that he didn't see as a mortal sin. He had a fear of hell because he felt he was sure to go there. After 45 minutes of talking with him and helping him get rid of his "make believe" mortal sins, I felt like a wash rag. I thought I did a good job that day, but the next day he was back with another load of mortal sins. Scrupulous people have an enormous parent, and you'd be amazed to what extent the "parent" is the chairman of the board in the lives of many average people.

Here are some examples of "parent" dictates and the stress they cause in people.

1. A woman's place is in the house

Dear Jim,
  It took me ten years before I felt good about working. I needed to work not only economically, but I, as a person, needed

stimulation. Today I have no guilt feelings because I was able to reassess my feelings. Today I say, "Yes, a woman's place is in the house, the House of Representatives, the State House, and the White House."
Sincerely,
Judy

2. You should act as a grown-up

Dear Jim,
Acting like a grown-up, whatever that is, really boxed me in. In school the rest of my class was having all the fun. Well, I'm 38 and finally acting like myself, and catching up with all the fun I missed when I was a teenager.
Sincerely,
Debbie

3. Men don't do housework

Annie Patrick, the woman who works with me on workshops, said this at a seminar entitled "Stress Reduction for Women in the Middle". "I did all the housework for my first 18 years of marriage. When I went to work I couldn't possibly do it all. I asked my husband to share the housework and he does. I have four kids, three of them are boys. I placed signs around the house that said, 'Mother doesn't work here anymore so clean up after yourself'. If I had my life to live over, I would have questioned this command 'Men don't do housework' long ago, and asked my husband & kids to share the burden."

4. Women should not like sex

I had a conversation with Louise at one of my marriage workshops. She told me, "From my upbringing, I picked up the idea that sex really wasn't much good, and God made it at a time when he was rushed and didn't have time to do a good job. I was a virgin when I got married. All of a sudden, on my honeymoon night, sex was supposed to be O.K. I couldn't switch gears that fast. It took me 12 years to realize that it is good and it is all right for women to enjoy sex. So right now I'm making up for lost time.

5. Salesmen are 2nd rate citizens

A middle-aged government employee told me that he hopes to go into sales. The following story shows how his parents had boxed him in. "From my family and friends I had been taught that technical positions were good and sales positions were bad. I am now computer-chief of my agency. However, I always wanted to be in sales. I am in sales part-time now and finally overcoming my parent scripting that 'sales work is bad'. I have fun being myself in the field of selling where talking to people delights me. It's much more personally rewarding than trying to build up a relationship with a computer."

6. Do it right or leave it alone

A business executive told me that he had many creative ideas but was always afraid to explore them or bring them out into the open for fear of making a mistake. "It really backfired on me. I repeatedly failed to make any suggestions at staff meetings because I was afraid I might be wrong and would not get promoted. Was I surprised when my evaluation stated that I was unimaginative! I was also not promoted. After that experience, I took a whole different outlook on making decisions. To make a mistake is human. In fact, I have probably learned as much from that mistake as from anything else. I've really reduced a lot of stress in my life since I've adopted a 'goof and grow' philosophy."

7. The less you reveal about yourself, the better off you will be

Lora, a teacher in my class, summed this whole thing up better than I can do.

Dear Jim,
 I sure grew up with a bunch of junk in the parent part of my personality. I grew up in the era with such commands as "Children are to be seen and not heard," "Don't wash your dirty linen in public," "Don't trust anyone," etc. I was in college before I realized that I never had a real friend. Friendship is impossible if you don't learn to share your feelings or trust anyone. I was taught to be shy and I've decided that shyness is not healthy. After much struggle and strife, I have some close friends who

have become the most rewarding part of my 'Me, Inc."
   Sincerely,
   Lora

In order to remove the parent from chairmanship of "You, Inc." you might have to do a lot of revamping. For instance, the following are a lot of common parental edicts that have stifled and caused stress in many people just like you.

   a. Your life is basically controlled by outside forces and you can't do much about it.
   b. Play it safe, don't take risks.
   c. Avoiding problems and letting time take its course is the best policy.
   d. It's either wrong or right.
   e. Make sure you please others before you think of yourself.
   f. Repressing negative feelings by picking up your cross and carrying it is the mark of the mature person.
   g. Always be right and be able to prove that others are wrong.
   h. Try to be good at everything or fake it until you make it.
   i. You should feel guilty if other people don't agree with your actions.

The adult has to be chairman of the board

In order to make "You, Inc." an effective organization you have to be the captain of your own ship. To become the captain of your own ship means the adult has to be the chairman of the board. This can be accomplished at any time in life that you choose to do it. For instance, I was in Durango, Colorado, a small mountain town, four years ago and I had just finished explaining the adult-parent-child to my class. I asked them to draw themselves 10 years ago and draw themselves today. A supervisor in the forest service came up with the following drawing.

A stressful life   **An enjoyable life**

He said, "In 1963 my parent was the chairman of my board. I was the Type A personality. I wanted to succeed. I was a hard worker and I had my own business. In fact, for seven years I worked seven days a week from 6:00 a.m. to 12:00 midnight. The only time I saw my children was when they were asleep. Then suddenly I began to question some of the parental edicts that I had inherited from church, family, and society. I was in stress up to my ears. After rethinking things for two months, I sold my construction business in California and moved to Durango, Colorado. For the first time I began to live. My wife loves it here. My boys and I ski, snowmobile and fish. We are surrounded by fresh air and just this year I finally am making what I was 10 years ago in my construction business." "Being" has become more important than "Having".

Notice the size of his child in his diagram of 1973. His child is really not chairman of the board. Actually in 1963 his parent was chairman of the board until his adult took over in 1973 and decided to spend more time taking care of the spontaneous, fun-loving, creative child. In this case and in many others, the parent is removed from control and the child profits.

Making your adult chairman of the board

If your "You, Inc." is going to function without a lot of distress, your adult will have to become the chairman of the board. If you are bombarded by "have to's", "ought to's", "must nots", and there is hardly any time in your "You, Inc." for "want to's" this could mean that you are boxed in and have a lot of distress. A simple way to assess your life is to write on a piece of paper all your activities in life under "ought to" or "want to".

OUGHT TO	WANT TO

If you are overloaded with things on the "ought to" side, it could very well indicate that your parent is chairman of your board. As long as the parent is in charge you have a built-in stress generator. You can use all the stress reducers from jogging to playing music, but the in-built parent generator will create more stress than you can ever handle with the best of stress reducing techniques.

If there is any stress generator that I know about, it is the "ought to" generator. In my nine years as a seminarian and my ten years as a priest, I had loads of "ought to's". For instance, "You must talk like a cleric." "You must set an example." "You must practice patience and repress your feelings." "What will the Bishop say?" "You must get permission from your superior." "Good priests wear their collars." "Good priests are not on the beach with teenagers until midnight." Here is how I would draw my life then.

The "ought to" part of my life as seminarian and priest

I learned to take all the "oughts" as God's will. Who was I to go against God's will? Then, Pope John came along and started questioning all the "oughts" with the words "We've got to open up the windows and let some fresh air in." From that time I have been trading my "ought to's" for "want to's". Finally, I got rid of my parent as chairman of the board and my adult is running "ME, INC." with far less stress and a lot more fun. Today I draw "Me, INC."

Switching to your adult as chairman

This sometimes frightens people. They think it means overthrow all of your responsibilities — be yourself and the hell with anyone else. If that were the case, the rebellious child would be chairman of the board of "You, Inc."

Last week I needed some real estate advice, so I met Craig in the bar after work. He is a manager of a big building firm in Denver. Aside from learning about real estate, I learned how he switched his "You, Inc." from the parent to the adult.

He had a job working with a government social agency in Iowa. The bureaucracy immobilized him. His parents told him to "stick it out." "You have a wife and child to support." His adult was pulling him in the direction of change by analyzing the situation. "I really began thinking. I hated my job; I weighed 250 pounds, and I was eating six packages of Di-Gel a day." He finally quit, left Iowa for Colorado, and has a challenging job which enables him to better support his family. He has lost 50 pounds and has not taken Di-Gel since he changed jobs.

Choosing your own "oughts"

For me, putting the adult in as chairman means choosing my own "oughts". I really have reduced stress and simplified my life with two oughts I choose from the adult. 1. I ought to do what I really like to do when that is possible. 2. I ought to be aware of others' rights. If doing what I want to do interferes or infringes on the rights of others, I don't do it or I do it at a time when it doesn't interfere. This is my simple norm of morality that works for me. By choosing my two "oughts" I automatically changed to the "wants" category, thereby removing the stress of "oughts" imposed by others.

I've had both experiences in my "Me, Inc." For years my parent was chairman of the board. Today my adult is chairman. I feel I have removed the greatest stress generator in my life. Lots of wonderful things have happened to me since my adult took over. I like myself much more. I enjoy life. I've learned to build better relationships with people. I make my own decisions which gives me a significant sense of worth. When I want to do something, I check it out with myself. If I think it is okay and it doesn't violate the rights of others, I do it and feel good about what I do. Today, my goal is helping people "like" themselves. I really believe that you can't like anyone unless you first learn to like yourself. Also, you will have a hard time liking yourself as long as the chairman of your "You, Inc." is your parent. If you have a lot of distress in your life due to an overload of "oughts" from your parent, who is chairman of the board, start a campaign to elect the adult as chairman. To do this, your campaign will consist of taking lots of time out to question your "oughts", to reassess your values, to re-evaluate and to try new behaviors to see if they fit you. It takes a lot of work and a lot of courage, but you can, with a little persistence and a lot of guts, remove this stress generator. Once you do, you will begin to know what joy it is just to **Have Fun Being Yourself**.

3. Do I have a communicational stress generator?

So far we have talked about the "doing, having, being" philosophical generators of stress. We have also talked about the "oughts", or psychological generators of stress. Now we will confront another "biggie". This is the stress generator hidden in our communicational relationships with others at work, in marriage, and teaching or raising children. The way we communicate with others is often definitely a generator of stress in ourselves and those around us.

Understanding the basic board members

Remember in your "You, Inc." you have three members — the parent, the adult, and the child. Everyone you meet has those

same three members. In order to grasp the relational stress generator you have to understand some basic characteristics of each part of "You, Inc."

Parent has two facets: a nurturing part: "Let me help you with your boots, Johnny;" and a critical part: "Put those boots on and stop complaining."

Adult has only a rational part: It is the thinking member of "You, Inc." that says, "Let's weigh the pros and cons." "Let's check out the cost of the new car against the cost of leasing a car."

Child has several parts: 1) Creative and spontaneous: "Yea, let's do it now." 2) Rebellious part: "Get off my back!" 3) Contemplative part: "I wonder what my Dad will say?"

There are more elaborate explanations of these three persons, but this is enough to know about them to understand the relational stress generator. In order to reinforce these basic concepts, try putting a P, A, or C after the following statements and compare your answers with those at the end of the exercise.

Exercise in identifying 3 persons in "You, Inc."

Each of the following ten situations is accompanied by one parent, one adult, and one child response. Place P, A, or C in each blank to indicate in which of the three persons in the "You, Inc." the response originates. Reading all three responses before answering might be helpful.

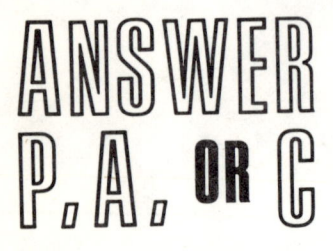

ANSWER P, A, OR C

Exercise in Identifying
3 Persons in "You, Inc."

1. The supervisor fills his extra large cup with coffee and puts a dime in the kitty.
   - ___ A. "You should pay 20 cents for as much coffee as you take."
   - ___ B. "He thinks HE is better than we are, but HE's not."
   - ___ C. "I wonder if he is aware that some resent his taking so much coffee for a dime?"

2. The ditto machine breaks down.
   - ___ A. "Would you call a repairman, Ms. Secretary?"
   - ___ B. "Nothing's the way it used to be, people just don't take pride in their work like they use to!"
   - ___ C. "Why does this always have to happen to me?"

3. A teacher finds a student smoking in the restroom.
   - ___ A. "You know its against the rules to smoke on school grounds!"
   - ___ B. "Are you aware of the rule against smoking on school grounds?"
   - ___ C. "Hey-y-y. I sure could use a drag off that cigarette."

4. A teacher's request to teach transactional analysis has just been refused.
   - ___ A. "He wouldn't even listen to MY side of the story."
   - ___ B. "I think the potential benefits derived from teaching T.A. are well worth the problems which might arise."
   - ___ C. "Anybody with any brains could see the value in teaching T.A. to students!"

5. Government workers are waiting for their agency meeting to begin.
   - ___ A. "I wonder what the nature of the meeting is?"
   - ___ B. "If he (the supervisor) thinks I'm going to sit here and listen to him tell us what a great supervisor he is, he's NUTS!"
   - ___ C. "We should have an agenda before every meeting."

6. John is late for work, another employee says.
   - ___ A. "You're late again. There must be something wrong with you."
   - ___ B. "If I were late, I bet I'd get fired."
   - ___ C. "The boss seems to be upset with John."
7. A very shapely young lady walks into the office wearing a tight jump suit.
   - ___ A. "Now that is out-a-sight."
   - ___ B. "What is she saying about herself by dressing in that manner?"
   - ___ C. "Anyone with an ounce of common sense wouldn't dress that way."
8. The bulletin reminds the workers that, "employees are required to stay in the building until 3:30, this means you."
   - ___ A. "**Who** does **he** think **he** is?"
   - ___ B. "It seems the supervisor is disturbed about some of us leavng early."
   - ___ C. "It's about time the LAW was laid down."
9. The faculty is discussing whether students should play chess during study hall.
   - ___ A. "Study hall is for studying, not playing."
   - ___ B. "What effect will allowing students to play chess have on the educational atmosphere of the study hall?"
   - ___ C. "I really fear the wrath of the angry parents of some of the students."
10. "You are without a doubt the worst supervisor I have ever had," says an angered employee.
    - ___ A. "I can see you are very angry with me and think I do not do what you expect me to do."
    - ___ B. "I have done everything I could possibly do for you. It's about time YOU GROW UP."
    - ___ C. "So, big deal, who cares!"

Answers:
1. P C A
1. A P C
3. P A C
4. C A P
5. A C P
6. P C A
7. C A P
8. C A P
9. P A C
10. A P C

Relational stress generators at work

If you have checked the right answers you have a good idea of the differences between the parent, adult and the child. Now you are ready to diagnose relational transactions between yourself and other people. They could be parent to parent, adult to adult, or child to child. However, if they are critical parent to child, then they are most probably stress generators. For instance, if your boss tells you, "Mildred, finish that job before 4:00 or you will stay until midnight," you seemingly are in a parent-child relationship and you could be collecting stress. If your boss habitually communicates with you this way, it could very well be a chronic stress situation.

The story of Lynn

Lynn is an executive secretary with the government with a GS 6 rating. She worked in a government agency in Denver. She was in a government workshop I was conducting for the Civil Service Commission. During the course of the class she analyzed her relational generators. For her it was her boss. He had an inaccurate self-image. He thought he was God. Any supervisor who has acquired the God image creates loads of stress. For instance, God knows everything, so why listen to his subordinates. God can't make a mistake, so others catch hell. Being single, she had clubs, parties, tennis and other stress reducers in her life, but her Godlike boss could create more stress than she could hope to reduce. She figured that she could not get her boss to leave the divinity and join the human race, so she left him. She resigned,

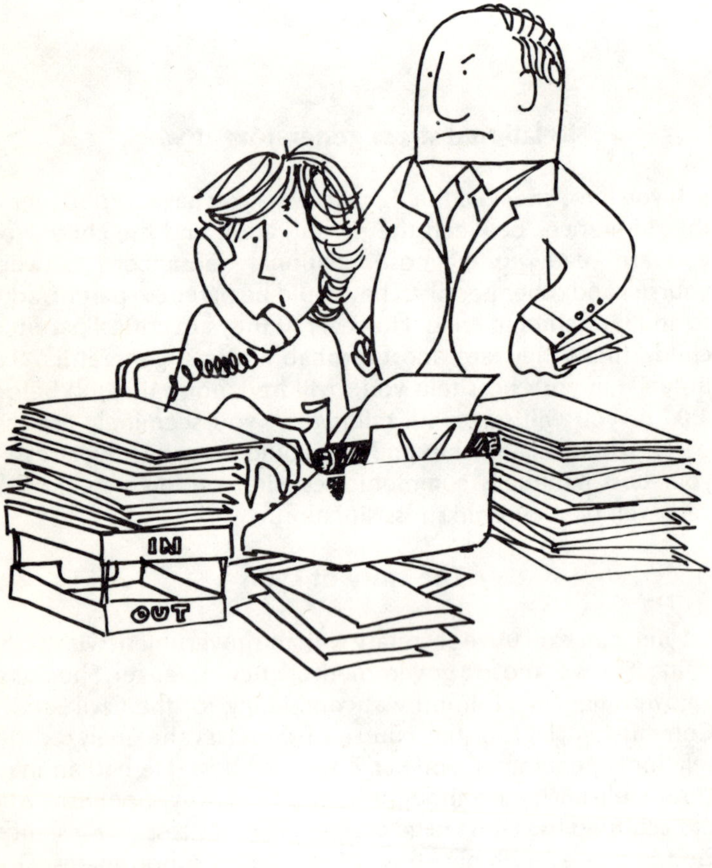
IN
OUT

took a downgrade, and went to Albuquerque. Going from a GS 6 to a 5 was really an upper for her. I had supper with Lynn. She is a changed person. She loves her job, her work, and her life. She broke a four-year parent-child relationship which was definitely a cause of stress. It may help to diagram the relational change Lynn made.

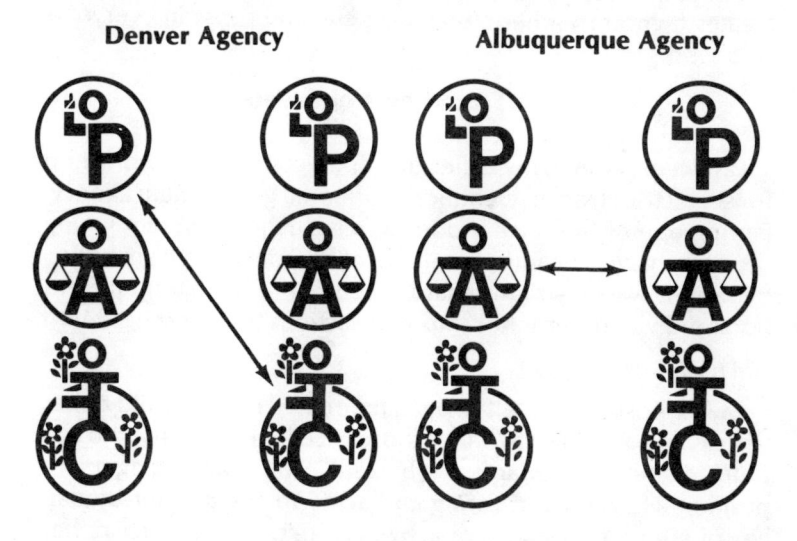

Denver Agency   **Albuquerque Agency**

From heaven to hell

Over the past several years, I have frequently visited friends in one particular government office. The boss was a super person who created beautiful adult-adult relationships. Visiting this office felt as warm and accepting as visiting blue Hawaii. Then came the turn about. This neat boss was transferred and his replacement, according to one of my friends in the agency, "should have been arrested for impersonating a human being". The blue skies turned to gray. The atmosphere literally switched from heaven to hell. I noticed it on my first visit under the new command. Everyone seemed uptight. It was about as much fun as visiting death row at San Quentin. Since this change of command several have quit and gone to work in the business world. Some have transferred and those who remain are overloaded with stress. Just last week I met a former employee of that agency. I said, "Virginia, you sure look good. You have lost ten pounds." She replied, "Jim, ever since I left my stress-generating boss I have felt like a new person. When I was working there I was always eating to get rid of the stress created by the dictator who took over as boss. In fact, occasionally I go out to visit my ex-inmates who are still imprisoned by the invisible bars of stress." This situation is typical when a supervisor has the attitude of " 'I'm okay,' everyone who works for me 'is not okay.' " This creates high atmospheric pressure, creating stress in everyone who works under it.

From hell to heaven

Last week, Annie, my colleague, and I conducted a workshop for secretaries from a scientifically oriented government agency. During one of the small group exercises Janet, a vibrant young secretary, gave a beautiful example of her transition from hell to heaven. It was so striking that I asked her to write it up for this book. I divided her letter into two sections, hell and heaven.

A. HELL

My ex-boss lacked self-image and treated me as a child rather than as an adult. He was one of those excellent scientists who was unfortunately "Upward Mobilized" into a management position. He was overbearing and acted totally disinterested in any of our section's work or activities. He dictated policy rather than inviting suggestions.

B. HEAVEN

My new boss believes in himself, in his own self-confident way so that he doesn't need to "prove" himself to anyone with overt aggressiveness, secretiveness, or power plays. He makes our office a cohesive unit which in turn results in a very smooth running operation. Every six months to a year, he has us all get together and discuss what we like about what we're doing, what we don't like, and how we can help each other in trading off jobs, etc. This includes everyone, no matter what their own title. My present job is the best thing that ever happened to me. I have a new sense of self-worth and self-image. My attitude has changed two-fold and now I love my career as a secretary because I now know how fulfilling it can be.

Janet

Talking to Janet and multitudes like her, I collected sets of Booster Statements or Killer Statements that are principal tools used by the two types of supervisors.

Killer phrases used by parent-child boss

a. "What bubble head thought that up?"
b. "I just know it won't work."
c. "Somebody would have suggested it before if it was any good."
d. "You'll never sell that to management."
e. "We've never used that approach before."
f. "They'll think we're long-haired."
g. "What will the customers think? They won't stand for it!"
h. "It's not our responsibility."
i. "It's not in the manual."
j. "Our people won't accept it."
k. "We can't do it under the regulations."
l. "Too modern."

Booster statements used by adult-adult boss

a. "Let's find out more about this."
b. "You've hit on a brilliant idea."
c. "Let's try it."
d. "That's good thinking."
e. "There's real possibility here."
f. "Excellent idea."
g. "Sit down - let's talk it over."
h. "Let's explore this further."
i. "We could use more of that type of thinking."
j. "You must have studied this problem."
k. "Sam came up with this idea."
l. "We have never done this before, let's try it."
m. "Nice work."
n. "That's planning ahead."

Booster statements give employees a sense of worth, dignity, and belonging. They open the door to creativity, high motivation, job satisfaction, and low distress levels. Killer statements, on the contrary, give employees an "I'm not okay" feeling. They create a high level of conformity, fear, and loads of distress.

Dave, the trainer of a huge engineering plant, told me they had three fatal heart attacks of men under 40 in one week. I asked why and he said, "Most people here hate their jobs, but the pay is so great that they are boxed in. The company has them in golden handcuffs. The company rewards a good engineer by making him a manager. They often end up losing a good engineer and gaining a lousy manager." One study indicates that the majority of managers in business tend to create this stressful parent-child atmosphere. Maybe this is because they reward faithful service in a technical field with a managerial position instead of searching for people with managerial ability.

Several years ago a study of "empathetic listening" was conducted by a doctoral student. He sampled students in every department at the university from drama to engineering. In empathetic listening, an essential managerial tool, scientists and engineers ranked below the 10th percentile even though I.Q.-wise they were in the top 10 percentile.

Perhaps this explains why it is so risky to reward a technically brilliant man with a managerial post. Better selection criteria and significant training could create better managers in business, education, and government and a lot less distress and job dissatisfaction among employees.

Marriage as a relational stress generator

In my younger days I still remember my girlfriend singing, with starry eyes, the song... "A honeymoon in Dallas and a brand new plastic palace... I'll buy that dream." Today it is "You Light Up My Life." Songs and our culture that still mislead young people into thinking that marriage is a haven of peace and the end of all distress. On the contrary, it is the most challenging relationship in the world. If your boss is a dictator, you can go home at 4:00. What do you do if you married a dictator?

What a letdown for the person going bright-eyed into marriage believing that his or her fiancee will light up all their tubes. Instead, they often find that a parent-child relationship takes place and one by one the tubes begin to be blown out.

Communication for survival

Last Thursday I went to a large cocktail party. I usually can take the chit-chat or small talk for about ten minutes, then I always create a significant encounter. I mentioned to a couple that I was working on stress reduction and they said, "That is what we need." They had six children, two from his first marriage and four of their own. I told them that Fran and I try to do the "Feeling Wheel" every morning so that we never collect stress.

They were super-interested and they wanted to make one. What you do is write four feelings you experienced in the last 24 hours — like this example.

FEELINGS WHEEL

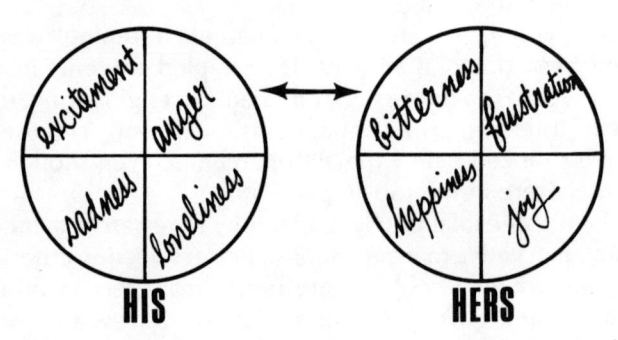

HIS: excitement, anger, sadness, loneliness ↔ HERS: bitterness, frustration, happiness, joy

When they finished we compared feeling-wheels. They both had anger.

His anger stemmed from the cold pancakes his wife made. Surprisingly enough, her anger was focused around the cold pancakes also. She said, "I tried to get Al up twice and he stayed in bed while I was up cooking and doing all the work. I felt cheated and angry. I could have put the pancakes in the oven, but I left them out to get even." As we discussed things they became clearer. She felt like a maid, his servant. He was so surprised. This is how his dad had always treated his mother.

Evident in this marriage was the hidden parent-child. She got even (the rebellious child) when she let the pancakes get cold. Imagine the distress in her, she feels like an overworked maid. The feeling wheel is a 24 hour safety valve which can allow each spouse to keep stress from becoming distress. Distress will "blow the marriage out of the saddle."

Divorce — a relational generator of stress

Divorce is hard and stressful. However, in an irreversible parent-child relationship, it cuts out the malignant stress generator. In Grand Junction, Colorado, at a government workshop, Flexible Fran and I spent time listening to a woman whose marital love had died 10 years ago because she was on the receiving end of a parent-child relationship and had been for 23 years. It took ten years to build up courage to admit that she goofed in her marriage and that now was the time to admit she had goofed and had begun to grow. She decided to file for divorce. Since I thoroughly covered divorce in my book **Re-entry Into the Single Life**, I'll conclude this section by sharing her recent letter with you.

Dear Jim,

I hardly know where to begin. First, I want you to know that I am very thankful that I was able to attend your class in Grand Junction even though my life has been turned upside-down since. The class has acted like a catalyst, creating a reaction of which I do not yet know the outcome. First of all, my husband cannot cope with me as an individual — "with my tubes lit up". I didn't realize how shaky he was in this area. I was even beginning to believe there had been growth in our marriage with both of us developing as individuals, rather than in the traditional parent-child relationship that had held us for so long. I know too well the frustration of being in a situation where one has to have permission to have an idea, even though the idea is always put down as some silly "woman's" notion. Anything learned and shared is put down with, "A little education is certainly a dangerous thing." Any apology, reaching out for communication and sharing of feelings — "I'm sorry" met with "You sure are".

My marriage has been a very frustrating and struggling experience. I am finally ready to admit I really goofed and I am ready to keep growing. I am determined to survive this chaotic breaking-up period.

Thanks,
Betty

SEE APPENDIX

Raising children - a relational stress generator

In a recent survey given to a number of American parents, an interesting question was asked. "If you had it to do over again, would you have children?" Over 50% responded negatively. As one fellow said, "I'm going to start a 'Rent-a-kid' firm to let newlyweds know what is involved in raising children." Coping with children is so important that we decided to do a special section on it. It is entitled "How to reduce stress in children and students" and it is the appendix of this book.

The hidden cause of relational stress

We have talked about relational stress generators in the essential playing field where life takes place . . . at work, in marriage, and in divorce. The basic cause of relational stress is the parent-child approach to communication. If we are in a parent-child relationship, we might well switch and stop bickering by making it an adult-adult relationship. If we are the distressful child in such a relationship, we may try to change it to an adult-adult . . . if that is impossible, we may consider cancelling the relationship and all the distress that goes with it. It is a gigantic job, but a journey of a thousand miles begins with one step. Are you ready to make that step?

4. Do I have a male-female hang-up stress generator?

The other day in the store I heard a mother telling her little boy who was crying, "Big boys don't cry." She is passing on the rules of being a boy — rules that will box in his feelings, rules that will later create high blood pressure, ulcers, and heart attacks.

Paul or Polly

To show you how unconsciously we are led or programmed along different paths — let's try the Paul - Polly twins' test.
After the statement, fill in Paul or Polly mentally or in writing.

POLLY OR PAUL?

1. This twin is dressed in pink at birth. _____
2. This twin helps Mom with the dishes. _____
3. This twin plays cowboys. _____
4. This twin plays dolls. _____
5. This twin is tough. _____
6. This twin likes flowers. _____
7. This twin likes motorcycles. _____
8. This twin dresses sloppy. _____
9. This twin always has perfect hair grooming. _____
10. This twin is emotional. _____

You probably scored 100%. Our society clearly stereotypes human beings according to definite male and female roles.

Who's number 1? Notice a girl can play cowboys and that is okay. She's a tomboy. What would happen if a boy wanted to play with dolls? Impossible! This could very well mean that males are No. 1 and females are No. 2 in our society. It is allowable for No. 2 to imitate No. 1, but totally against the rules for No. 1 to imitate No. 2. Both men and women are programmed, while growing up, into Paul or Polly behaviors. These stereotyped roles generate loads of stress.

If you have your choice, be born a male

In an article in "New Woman", June, 1977, Donald Smith relates the story of how the woman role of Wanda literally imprisoned her. The situation is this: A man was left with four sons and one daughter to raise after his wife died. The father was pretty well off financially, but he decided that his daughter, Wanda, was to assume the role of her late mother. She was taken from school at the age of 16 and became a Cinderella without a prince. Her four brothers attended college, married, and became businessmen, leaving her to attend to her aging father. When she was in her 40's her father died, leaving her 1/5 of his estate. She went to work and supported herself till she died at the age of 70. She never questioned this burden she had inherited; she merely accepted it as an obligation, as an infallible "ought".

What a tragic misfortune it was for her to be born a female. If only she could have seen herself as a human instead of as a female ... if only she had had the courage to tell her father and four brothers that she had rights also ... if only she could have stood up for those rights as a human being ... what a different life she could have led. It is too late for her but not for you.

Researchers are finding out that it doesn't pay to be a "macho" male or a super "thoroughbred" female. Those who take on the rigid male role or female role seemed to acquire more distress, more high blood pressure, heart attacks, and other psychosomatic illnesses. Since we are a combination of our father and our mother, it seems that we would have less stress if we spent most of our energies on being human rather than rigidly male or female. Those in the field of "Androgyny" (you'll have to look that one up) say that men should be gentle and women should be assertive. They contend that a man should be emotional, warm, kind, and that women should be frank and straight-forward. They are saying that qualities which we have assigned specifically to male or female should be merely human qualities . . . and the fully human person (man or woman) would do well to develop all human qualities. Not being "male or female", but being fully human is the key to removing the "boxing in" of the male-female role generator.

Men in need of liberation

I grew up as a tough guy. In fact, I beat up other kids to prove that I was not "chicken". As I look back, I was actually chicken because I didn't want to beat up anyone, but did it because I was afraid that the other tough guys would call me "chicken". Boy, what an anxiety and stress creating trip the "tough guy" and "big boys don't cry" syndrome was for me. This trip is still being laid upon the future "macho males".

How can men build a deep relationship when society says it is a sign of weakness for men to express feelings? How can men know themselves if they don't feel free to express their real feelings?

The impotent male

On one of the early morning talk shows the host was interviewing a psychologist who conducted feeling therapy for men. He said that a significant number of men in the U.S. become impotent. They (along with our Type A culture) connect "doing" or "performance" with their self-image. If they can't perform one time in sex, they become super-anxious. The anxiety makes them repeat their non-performance. Who can they tell? Going to a counselor is hard because being a man means "being able to solve your own problems" and it is a weakness to ask for help. You can see how imprisoned many men are. They are actually in the invisible prison of the male role.

Using "macho male" for gain

A middle-aged man decided he wanted to buy a new Thunderbird. Before he signed the papers he said, "Wait, I'd better call my wife to get her okay. She handles the books." The shrewd salesman said, "Wait, maybe I'd better call my wife to get her okay to sell it to you." Needless to say, he sold the car and the buyer didn't call his wife. This salesman was aware of the "macho male" cultural role.

Henpecked or not?

In one marriage class we had a big debate. Two wives said that they wanted their husbands to call on Fridays if they stayed for the late "Thank God it's Friday drinks." The husbands felt that calling would put them in a subordinate role. Their greatest fear, however, was the other fellow saying, "Charlie is calling his wife .

. . I didn't know he was henpecked."

This reminds me of a story at Peter's pearly gates. At one gate was a long line of men. It was the gate where the wives had been the bosses. The other gate was for those fellows who were the bosses. Joe noticed Henry, his next door neighbor, in the wrong line. He shouted, "Henry, you weren't the boss, what are you doing there in that line?" Henry turned around and replied, "My wife told me to shut up and get in this line."

Relationally impotent

The impotence in creating a deep relationship is even more widespread than physical impotence. Last summer a beautiful woman said her 25 year old daughter just broke up with her boyfriend because he was imprisoned in the rigid role of the male and just could not express his feelings. She wrote this poetic song for him.

Oh my friend and dearest lover
if there was only one gift I could give,
I'd rouse all the feelings dormant in you,
teach you that to feel them is to live.

Oh my friend and dearest lover,
let me show you what it is to cry.
To shatter the hurt into rivers,
and let it flow until they run dry.

Oh my friend and dearest lover,
I know you were told it was wrong.
You had to hide your feelings on the pretense
that a man must be cold to be strong.

CHORUS:
For if you don't deal with the things that you feel
then you're only half alive and always reaching.
If you won't deal with all that you feel
you'll miss most the lessons life is teaching.

Oh my friend, my lover,
I know it's hard for you to show you care,
to crack away the years that bind you
and let another person know what's there.

*But, oh, my friend and lover,
please don't let the past force you to see
only a part of the person
that's inside of you and struggling to be.*

— Marla Schoer

I think men can break through their roles and join the human race. It may take awhile but it's happening every day. Not everyone shares my optimism.

Possible but not probable

Dear Jim,

My goal in life is to see men become liberated. I feel it is such a tragedy that men have been brought into this world truly believing that they are not to show emotion, share feelings, and sadder yet, commit themselves.

The man with whom I am in love is the typical unliberated man. We just can't communicate when it comes to personal problems. He will not share his feelings; rather, puts on the facade of the hassle-free, easy-going, lucky man. I'll have to admit he hides his emotions (sad) well, but I'm not fooled by his front.

I would give anything just to see him **totally** release himself. He has a problem of trust, which invades his desire to be open and share himself.

Is there anyone working on ways to liberate men? I'm aware of group therapies; however, few men will attend. When will the day come when men don't feel belittled by crying, sharing and loving?

I hope I am still around when a man can cry on my shoulder!!

Through your course, I became aware that it is **possible** to liberate men, yet not **probable**.

Sincerely,
Paula

5. Do I have a role identity stress generator?

In my view, nothing is more powerful in creating stress in your life than the role vs. identity generator. As I have said before, a major goal in my life is to create atmospheres in which people can know themselves, like themselves, and have fun being themselves. The market for this product in our role-immersed world is overpowering. In my class on "Enhancing Self-Concept" (a high-class name for "Having Fun Being Yourself"), I have asked literally hundreds of people to write the answer to the question — who am I? I ask them to write it ten times. Ninety-five per cent of all answers are roles, e.g., father, mother, engineer, secretary, teacher, etc. What do roles tell you about the person? Nothing! They do tell you that most people are heavy on roles and light on identity.

Let's go a little deeper. Our society rewards people for being somebody (roles). How many fathers have said, "Son, I went to the eighth grade; you go to college and be somebody"? Have you ever heard of a dad saying, "Son, try to find out who you are and then decide what you want to do in life"? How many schools in America give an award for "Being Yourself"? Remember the National Honor Society rewards a grade point average (doing). Our high school gave awards for perfect attendance (doing). Again, behind the scenes we see the predominant philosophy of doing and having. Being (identity) comes in last. Is it any wonder that over 70% of college graduates change their field in five years after college? Is it any wonder that so many people who retire are often dead in five years? Their identity was their role. They lost their role and became nobodies.

A brilliant young man in pre-med school at Boston College was getting all "F's". A wise counselor asked his parents to come out for a conference. They found that he didn't want to become a doctor but was doing it to please them. His dad was a doctor and there was a line of doctors in the family going back to Abraham. The counselor had a knack of creating an atmosphere in which the young man felt free to express his real feelings. He found out that the fellow loved math and was intrigued with engineering. As a result of that one meeting all agreed that he should be himself. He switched to engineering; his grades went up; he enjoyed school; and he was "Having Fun Being Himself" instead of trying to live his life for his parents.

Some of the exciting things about my field of creating atmospheres, in which people can search out who they are and go anywhere they want, are peak experiences I have had in doing my hobby, which is also my job.

Three months ago I had such a peak experience. Kathy worked in the child abuse center at Colorado General Hospital. She came to see Annie and me about doing a workshop for the paraprofessionals in the child abuse clinic. We decided that she should sit in on an upcoming class so she could decide whether or not this approach would fit her needs.

Well, she spent one day in class and that one day changed the direction of her whole life. In one day, there was a change in her chairman of the board . . . the parent was ousted and her adult took over. What happened? She made a $36,000 decision. She had enrolled at D.U. for the Social Studies program and she was going to get her Masters. Why? "Because I had my role and identity really confused. I was getting a degree because the parent part of "Me, Inc." was telling me that I "ought to". You see, my dad was a medical doctor; my brother is a doctor at the Mayo Clinic; my sister has her Ph.D. in medicine and gives talks around the country. I felt that I ought to do (DOING) the same thing so I would have a degree (HAVING) like the rest of my family . . . but I was not being myself. I don't want a degree nor do I want to be a social worker. I love the theatre . . . and also, I want to open up a T-shirt business where I design and sell T-shirts." What happened? She resigned from grad school and lost her $100 registration fee. However, she saved $36,000... the price it would have cost her to get through grad school, including the loss of two years' wages. She adds, "I think my marriage would have collapsed while I was going to grad school because I was putting extra pressure on my husband. I was so unhappy doing what I felt my parents wanted instead of doing what I wanted in my life.

Two months ago, I went to see "Godspell" at Eugene's Theatre in Denver. One of the leads was Kathy. She performed superbly. She found her place. She is now in the theatre full time and still has her T-shirt business in mind. What a rewarding experience it was for me to view Kathy "being herself", bubbling with happiness. I like to think that I had a hand in creating an atmosphere which helped Kathy break through a prison of roles, so that she could find who she was and what she wanted to do with her precious gift of life. Four months ago she was overloaded with the liability of stress. Today her "You, Inc." is blooming and growing and her stress level is way down. Her satisfaction level is way up. Kathy was able to make the following anonymous poem come alive in her life:

*If you could really accept
that you weren't ok
you could stop proving you were ok.*

*If you could stop proving
that you were ok
you could get that it was ok not to be ok.*

*If you could get that it was ok not to be ok
you could get that you were ok the way you are.
You're ok, get it?*

The story of a fire prevention chief

John is a close friend of mine. Like almost everyone else, he became caught up in the role-oriented world. He always wanted to be a fireman. However, after 17 years on the job he ran into a role identity conflict. He was selected from 12 district chiefs to be the fire prevention chief, which is really a "status" job on the fire department.

He spent 18 months on the job and he collected a lot of stress. He started to bring his job home and increased his drinking to drown the newly created stress.

He came face to face with a role-identity conflict. Some politicians put pressure on the chief to permit their friends to omit some of the fire codes in their buildings. The big chief put pressure on John to overlook the big boys. John saw himself as a square shooter. "If the ordinary fellow has to abide by the law, so should the big-shot friends of the politicians." He was talking about things that are essential for life safety. He said, "I have to sleep at night. I can't sleep if I clear an unsafe building." The chief told him to clear it. He told the chief to clear it himself. The battle was on. John decided he couldn't keep the role of fire prevention chief and be true to his identity as a person. He resigned and is back in the district. He fought the stressful battle of role and identity. He won because he was true to himself. He has given up the prestigious role of fire prevention chief, but he has safeguarded his identity. He lived Shakespeare's maxim "To thine own self be true and thou can't be false to any man."

A word from the dream world

Recently, I've gone to several dream analysis workshops. I find them intriguing. The theory is that dreams are our subconscious giving us messages on how to become more ourselves. This one woman reported a dream she had had several years ago. It concerned being held by the Nazis and she had awakened terrified. Jeff, the analyst, said that ROLE THINKING IS NAZI THINKING. Some role in her life was keeping her from being herself and she was afraid to step out of that role. The woman was amazed. "That fits me perfectly. I was in the housewife role for 17 years. I was frightened to death to go out into the real world. Actually, returning to school was my turning point and the first decision I have made. Since then, I don't have those Nazi nightmares."

You may not agree with the dream interpretation, but hopefully you can see how roles can smother people and prevent them from the stimulating world of being themselves.

Identity-role has its troubles

Someone once said, 'Blessed are the thieves who stole my masks." When you drop roles and start becoming yourself, your "You, Inc." begins to hit on all eight cylinders. However, the change will have repercussions on those around you. Listen to the letter from Phyllis.

Dear Jim,

My husband married a clinging vine. I hung on his every word and his decisions for years. He wouldn't even let me help paint the walls in the house because he didn't think I could do it right. He is a geologist for the government and for many years the kids and I went with him to the field for three months each summer. This was a fun time and we all enjoyed the close family relationships. Then he was assigned to a spring-fall field season and we all couldn't go because of school commitments. I then had to be mother and father for six to eight weeks at a time and make all the decisions of running the family. My independence and self-assurance increased by leaps and bounds. Not too long after, I returned to substitute teaching. I also started other interests outside the home. Now I have a reasonably good feeling about myself. However, my husband's self-concept has been shaken. For a long time he couldn't understand how I could change from such a weak, quiet wife to one who could manage the house and five girls when he was gone. I also had thoughts and ideas on raising the girls and the spending of our money. He is still working on this problem and hopefully in the near future he'll finally realize that there can be two thinking, loving, and happy adults in a marriage. Maybe I should talk him into taking your self-concept class.

    Jill

Francine puts it all together in her poem, "I AM MINE":

When I was first born I was
  my mother's baby.
When I was small,
  my father's little girl.
Teenage years made me
  my boyfriend's sweetheart
Marriage made me
  my husband's wife.
Until uncertainty let me go
  and I belonged to no one
  and I was nothing.
Trial and turmoil resulted
  until the day I realized

*Only I see with these eyes
   smell with this nose
   taste with this mouth
   and feel with these feelings.
Since that moment
   I share my thoughts and body
   with whom I wish
   But I belong to no one*

I am mine.
          — Francine Fuerst

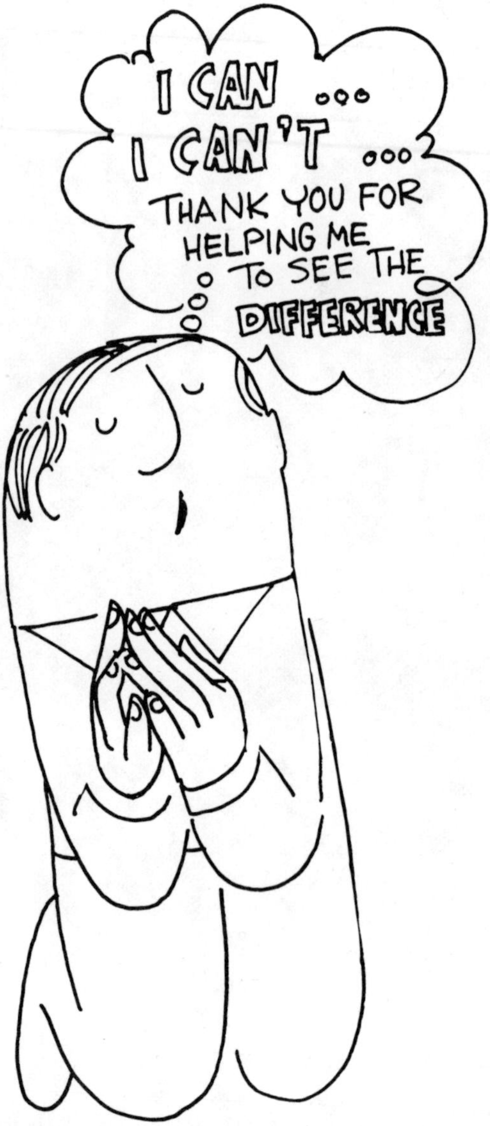
I CAN ...
I CAN'T ...
THANK YOU FOR HELPING ME TO SEE THE DIFFERENCE

CHAPTER VIII

WHERE DO I BEGIN?

We have been kicking around the idea of a powerful and relevant stress reduction tool that people could use in their everyday life. When John Roughan and I were in the seminary together, we meditated for one hour every morning as part of the schedule. Meditation means taking a look at your life and reassessing your values. It is probably one of the most powerful tools to keep your company, "You, Inc." in the business of creating a fulfilling life. Actually, meditation means that every day you have a board meeting. At this meeting the adult is chairman of the board. As chairman he evaluates the direction that your parent wants to go and the direction that your child wants to go. Keeping harmony between the demands of the parent and the spontaneity of the child is the way to reduce stress in "You, Inc."

Begin with this basic tool

Here is a basic tool for coping with stress. It is summed up well by this three-part prayer:

1. Lord, give me the serenity to accept those things I cannot change;
2. the courage to change those things I can;
3. and the wisdom to know the difference.

If your "You, Inc." has a regular meeting and makes use of this practical stress-coping tool in your everyday life, you will find the assets of happiness going up and the liabilities of distress decreasing in your business of "You, Inc." Let's see how this works in everyday life.

The flat tire

One morning on the way downtown my left rear tire went flat. I don't like to change tires and ordinarily this produces stress. First of all I had to accept the unchangeable fact that the tire had no air in it (accepting things I cannot change). However, I could change my attitude toward the flat tire (changing those things I can change). That is exactly what I did. I like to keep in condition and to do workouts, so I viewed the episode as a mini-workout. Viewing it as good exercise, I changed my attitude toward a potentially stressful incident. I almost enjoyed it and I certainly minimized stress.

Driving in traffic

Driving in traffic has always caused stress in me as well as in millions of Americans. Five years ago I was talking to Jerry, a teacher at Colorado University. I was commenting on how frustrating it must be to drive daily from Denver to Boulder in all that traffic. He said to me, "Oh no, it is not frustrating at all. I look forward to it because it gives me time alone to do some thinking." Since that time I incorporated that idea into "Me, Inc." I figured that I have to accept driving in traffic because I can't change that reality. So, I changed my attitude toward it. Like Jerry, I now use my time driving for my board meetings of my "Me, Inc." This has decreased stress and increased happiness in my life by switching me from a Type A to a Type B driver.

The domineering boss

Rosemary, a secretary for HEW, said, "My boss thinks he is God's gift to humanity. He gave me a high level of stress every time I had to go into his office. He seemed to put himself way above me and made me feel like a nobody. One of my friends said that every time I had to go into the office, I should picture him sitting there in his underwear. I tried that two years ago and it worked wonders for me. Instead of high level fear, I find myself inwardly giggling." Rosemary accepted the fact that she could not change her boss. She reduced the liability of fear and stress and increased her enjoyment at work by changing her attitude toward him — just by a simple technique of picturing him sitting there smoking a cigar in his underwear.

Christmas shopping

For most people, buying Christmas gifts is something they cannot change. For Dolores, this creates real stress. What does she do to reduce it? She can't change the necessity of buying gifts, so she changes her approach to Christmas shopping. She goes shopping with a good friend. They have lunch at an elegant restaurant, the baby sitter has the kids, and all this is turned into a fun experience instead of a stressful situation. She "changed those things she could change."

Writing a book

My hobby is people. I work with people all over the country. I learn so much from listening to them either during the seminars or over a drink afterwards. To share what I learn from people, I know I have to write. For me, locking myself up in a room to write a book is stressful. It is unbelievable how the stress is turned into enjoyment when I write a book together with my life-long friend, John Roughan.

Job boredom

Many Americans suffer from job boredom. They are unsatisfied, unfulfilled, or feel unneeded. John Westine, a friend of mine, now works for the Bureau of Standards. Before that he was in a situation where he was very bored with his job. He happened to attend a reality therapy seminar and was told by the leader to change those things he could. Next day he told his boss that he didn't like his job. The following Monday his boss offered him another job, one that challenged his talents and also allowed him to attend graduate school again. John says boredom sets in at the point where "you accept something less than you think you deserve." One of the basic suggestions John has for job boredom is what he calls the Goya principle. GOYA stands for GET OFF

THE GOYA PRINCIPLE "GET OFF YOUR ASS"

YOUR ASS. By being assertive and telling people what you want, you are taking a step in the right direction. Here again, you have the choice of changing a part of your life which might cause you stress by changing jobs or by trying something to add vitality to your present job.

Changing a marriage

Working in communication and marriage provides me with many examples of how people can reduce stress by making significant changes. Listen to Betty Ann. "I got married twenty years ago when a women's worth depended totally on her husband. My husband was Mr. Big Man in the government. For 15 years I felt that I was his maid. I was in a parent-child situation. I was so busy raising four children that I didn't realize how stressful this relationship was. When I wanted to become a person instead of 'his wife', he said I was going through the change of life. To get his attention, I separated for a year. Today, we have an enjoyable adult-adult marriage instead of the stressful parent-child marriage." She changed the thing she could change.

Happily divorced

Several weeks ago after class, Julia wanted to talk with me. Her story really brings out the last part of the stress reduction formula — The Wisdom to Know the Difference. Here's her story. "For ten years I lacked the wisdom to know the difference. My marriage died ten years ago but I guess my parent was chairman of the board. I felt that I couldn't get a divorce. I grew up with parents who never allowed a mistake. Also inside my 'Me, Inc'. was the command, 'You made your bed, lie in it.' Now that I've made the decision to leave I feel like all the stress is being lifted, just like the clouds opened and the sun came bursting through. My adult took over as chairman of the board and the stock in my 'Me, Inc.' is really on the rise and paying dividends. If I would have had the simple tool 'to accept those things you cannot change, change those you can, and the wisdom to know the difference,' I would have saved ten years of life. I'm glad I finally did it. Maybe my story will help others trade in their stress for happiness."

Twenty-one ways to cope with your principal stress generator

What is the principal generator of stress? By now you probably have figured it out. That's right! It is YOU. Once you see that "my mother-in-law makes me feel guilty" can be replaced with "I let my mother-in-law make me feel guilty," you will realize that it is not others who cause your stress but your letting them. You can't change others but you can change your attitude toward them. THAT IS THE KEY.

What better investment of your time is there than spending most of it in a profitable return - in changing what you alone can change, YOURSELF? To do this, we have made a self-analysis thermometer. A doctor will check out your physical health by a thermometer. You can check out your stress-coping health by rating yourself on the checklist of attitudes or qualities you need to be "stresslessly" healthy. Let's face it, the mentally healthy person can cope with stress better than anyone else. Rate yourself twice on this checklist: (1) where you are; and (2) where you want to be. The scale goes from a low of one to a high of ten.

```
        A                    B
|___|___|___|___|___|___|___|___|___|___|
 0   1   2   3   4   5   6   7   8   9   10
```

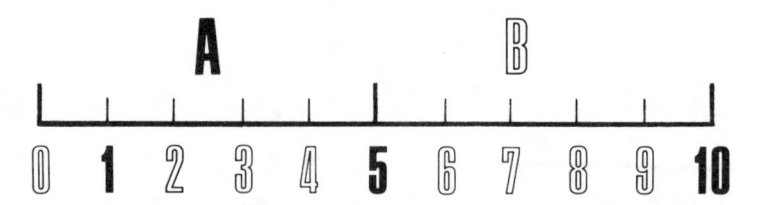

In the above example, A is where you are and B is where you want to be. You can change your "You, Inc." by setting a goal to get yourself from A (where you are) to B (where you want to be).

Now that we have the rules, let's start working on your greatest stress generator, YOURSELF.

1. HOW MUCH DO I LIKE MYSELF?

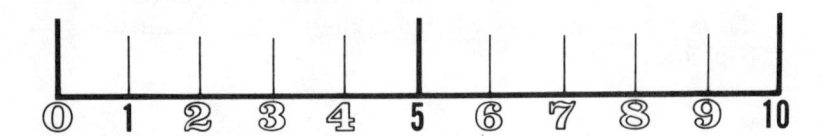

```
|___|___|___|___|___|___|___|___|___|___|
 0   1   2   3   4   5   6   7   8   9   10
```

I can't remember when or where, but a fellow told me, "Jim, Christ said to 'Love Thy Neighbor As Thyself', and we have forgotten the 'As Thyself' part." I wholeheartedly agree with that. When I was growing up I got the feeling that God really goofed when he made us. He apparently had worked for six days straight with no coffee breaks and He was really tired when He (or She) created us. Now I firmly believe that loving yourself is not only unselfish, but you really cannot love anyone unless you learn to love yourself first. Notice the word learn. **We learn mental health.** We learn to love ourselves. You'd be surprised how many people don't really like themselves.

A 43 year old secretary in the National Park Service gave me a big hug at the end of the fifth day of a workshop and said to me, "Jim, as a result of this workshop, I learned to like myself for the first time in my life." Unfortunately a lot of people don't like themselves at all (those who do could learn to like themselves more).

The following little quiz on how well you like yourself is not perfect, like any other psychological measure, but it is profitable as well as enjoyable. It was adapted from Dr. David Viscount's

"Are You the Kind of Person You'd Like to Know?" Try it, you may like it!

"Getting to know and like yourself"

Your feelings about yourself influence your feelings about almost everybody and everything else. Your self-image affects your judgement. It may lead you to be overly pessimistic and to miss many opportunities because you feel hopeless about yourself. Or it may lead you to act too optimistically and foolishly court disaster because you feel like you helped God with the creation of the world.

We all have our ups and downs, but generally our feelings lie somewhere in the middle.

The following 50 statements could be said about all of us from time to time. Indicate how often each statement would hold true for you by giving it the following marks:

HOW OFTEN?
0 - NEVER
1 - RARELY
2 - OCCASIONALLY
3 - USUALLY
4 - ALWAYS

1. I feel important.
2. If someone hurts my feelings I let them know.
3. I'm optimistic.
4. I enjoy shopping for clothes.
5. I like looking at myself in a full-length mirror.
6. My weight is approximately where I want it.
7. I like being seen at parties.
8. I enjoy being seen in a bathing suit.
9. I feel well dressed.
10. If I were a member of the opposite sex, I would find me attractive.
11. I don't bear grudges.
12. Nothing is too good for me.
13. I feel intelligent.

14. I can laugh at my own mistakes.
15. I enjoy sex.
16. I'm energetic.
17. I'm in a good mood.
18. It takes a lot to discourage me.
19. People value my opinions.
20. I can hold my own in a conversation.
21. I enjoy meeting and talking to new people.
22. Others like me.
23. I can do almost anything I really set my mind to.
24. I feel I'm in control of my destiny. The adult is chairperson of the board of "Me, Inc."
25. There's not much about me that I'd honestly like to change.
26. If I ever got in trouble, my friends would be there to help.
27. I've got a style that's clearly my own.
28. Most of the people I meet are worse off than I.
29. I've done little that worries me.
30. Others need me.
31. I can take care of myself.
32. My life is full.
33. It would be hard to replace me.
34. I love getting up in the morning.
35. Luck plays a part in my life.
36. I'm a kind person.
37. I'm not in a rut.
38. I feel I'm still growing.
39. People don't ordinarily take me for granted.
40. I don't let others push me around.
41. I like to confide in people.
42. I really enjoy my work.
43. I like where I live.
44. I've accomplished a great deal.
45. My life has been rather interesting.
46. If I had my life to live over, I wouldn't really change much.
47. There's little I'm ashamed of.
48. There aren't many people I would switch places with.
49. I seldom blame myself for anything.
50. Others generally admire me.

Add up your score and see if you really like yourself.

SCORE OF 160 OR MORE

You're terrific if you are as good as you think you are. Should your score be 175 or higher, however, you are probably exaggerating your self-worth so much that you distort the world around you.

Not too many people feel as good about themselves as you do. If you're presently in the process of falling in love, or have just won a lottery, your temporarily inflated self-image is probably understandable. Other people who feel as you do, however, are unrealistic and rigid, removed from the feelings of others.

You are possibly too self-involved, too inconsiderate of others' feelings and overly concerned with your own. You may often try to block out unpleasant feelings, especially sad ones, and may have a hard time admitting failure or loss. You cope with failure in one area by quickly trying to succeed in another, or by pretending you don't care.

To show greater interest in other people's lives is your need, especially in those areas that do not relate to your own interests. You frequently turn people off by appearing interested only in yourself. When you tell them how terrific you are, most people don't believe you. They see you merely running away from conflicts. If you learn to accept your own limitations and failures, you'll find you are not as good as you may want to be, but not as bad as you fear you are either.

SCORE OF 130-159

An optimistic realist, you certainly have a healthy view of yourself. You have energy, pride, and ambition. Since you hate to be pushed around and react quickly to protect your rights, it's difficult for anyone to take advantage of you. You are industrious, and generally get what you want because you work hard to correct any mistakes.

This analysis may sound like a prediction from a fortune-telling machine, but in fact these are the characteristics of someone with a high self esteem. Those who score this way do have many good things to be said on their behalf. You feel entitled to succeed; you accept responsibility for your own success and work at it. What you dislike about yourself you try to change. The only advice for you: keep it up!

SCORE OF 100-129

You tend to sit back and do little about the things you don't like although much of the time you have a good opinion of yourself and your activities. It's not that you don't see what's wrong - you are very realistic. It's just that you don't believe enough in yourself or think you deserve additional attention. In short, you don't think you are good enough to achieve more happiness through your own efforts.

If you learn to change certain attitudes about yourself, you can be happier. You see yourself as a thoughtful, decent, kind person, and interested in others. You can continue to feel that way and still learn to put yourself first more of the time. Try to make yourself more the center of the stage - assert your rights! Stop giving in so much; don't allow events just to happen without your influencing them. You can have more control over your life than you believe, but planning and effort are required. Create higher goals for yourself.

SCORE OF 70-100

You have a low self-image and you already know that. If you've recently experienced some loss or defeat, this may explain your score. Losses make everything appear black, just as windfalls create a rosy glow.

Nevertheless, you feel tired, stressful, empty, worthless much of the time. Perhaps you also feel trapped and are angry and "guilty". Not much of a socializer, you are not pleased with most of what you are doing at the present.

Your present situation needs to be re-thought. When was the last time you felt really good about yourself? What happened to make you change that opinion? Are there steps you could take now that would make your life better? Perhaps your life-plan simply had a major setback and you lost faith in yourself.

SCORE OF LESS THAN 70

Beyond a doubt you need help! Your self-opinion is unrealistically gloomy. You feel depleted, isolated and distressful. No use listing everything that's wrong - all you want is to feel better. If no major disappointment in your life is causing your gloom just now, you should try to find a professional who can help you out with some therapy. Changing your life begins by doing something, making a step. Don't delay. Do it **now**. The very act of taking one step will significantly reduce stress in your life.

How did you like the "Liking Yourself Quiz"? You don't have to agree with the results; however, if you want to "come alive" and live life to the fullest, you'll have to buy into the reason for the quiz. This is, to start you thinking how important it is to "know thyself" and "like thyself."

2. HOW OPTIMISTIC AM I?

```
0  1  2  3  4  5  6  7  8  9  10
```

Two teenagers were at a party and they found an unclaimed bottle of wine that was half full. George said, "Gee, it is half empty." Bob shouted, "Wow, it's half full." The same half bottle brought disappointment to George and happiness to Bob.

There was a mother with twin boys. She went to a child psychologist to ask his advice on how to balance out the two twins. Tommy was a total pessimist and Ronny was a total optimist. He told her to try this, "For Christmas, buy Tommy a room full of the best toys money can buy. Give Ronny a big box of horse manure." She did and Christmas morning she looked in on Tommy and he was saying, "These toys are no good; they're not what I wanted; they won't last." Then she went into Ronny's room and he was digging his way through the horse manure saying, "You can't fool me, where there's manure there's got to be a pony." The song "You've Got to Accentuate the Positive, Eliminate the Negative," reflects the optimistic attitude so necessary to cope with stress.

3. DO I HAVE FRIENDS?

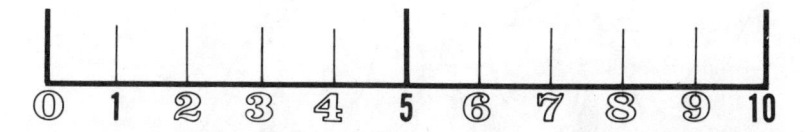

```
0  1  2  3  4  5  6  7  8  9  10
```

The other day I was visiting a friend Pete, who in the eyes of others is an important administrator at the university. In his own eyes his university status was spelled out by the plaque on his desk. It said, "I must be a mushroom, they keep me in the dark and feed me lots of horseshit." You may feel like a mushroom at work, at home, or other places, but if you have learned the art of making friends, you'll create a happy little mushroom out of yourself.

Friendship is no fringe benefit for your "You, Inc." Let's face it, you need others to become yourself . . . and the song is right, "People Who Need People Are the Luckiest People in the

World."

James Lynch in his book, **The Broken Heart: The Medical Consequence of Loneliness**, contends that loneliness will put you in a higher death rate than those who learned the art of making friends. He claims that dialogue with friends is the "elixir of life." This doesn't mean you have to be married. It does mean that you need friends with whom you can share your feelings.

Let's connect it with the number one killer — stress. Type A people, he contends, are often workaholics and consequently tend to be isolated from their mates and their families. Actually, when married they are "married singles."

So, if you prefer to stick around awhile and "put off dying until the very end", you may want to sharpen your skills of enriching your present friendships and creating new ones. One of my most rewarding hobbies is making new friends. Try it, you may love it.

4. DO I HAVE A SENSE OF HUMOR?

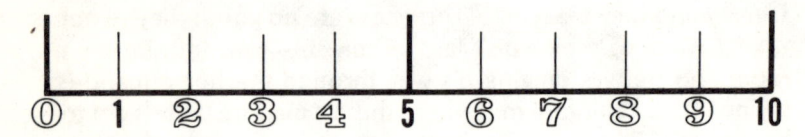

0 1 2 3 4 5 6 7 8 9 10

A person who has a real sense of humor, to me, is one who is able to laugh at himself. Dr. Murray Banks tells the story of a man staying at a resort in upstate New York. There was a lake on part of the huge property where he could go swimming in his birthday suit. While he was swimming some practical jokers stole his clothes. All he could find was an old hat to cover himself. As he approached the lodge, an elderly Jewish lady began to bend over with laughter. He angrily said, "If you were a lady, you wouldn't laugh." She retorted, "And if you were a gentleman you would tip your hat." Now there's a lady with a sense of the ridiculous. Did you know that you can't be angry and laugh at the same time? The power of humor will dissipate the lethal effects of stress in your life.

One way to liven up a monotonous sermon

A long-winded priest was giving a sermon on the island of Kaui in Hawaii. After 35 minutes, a woman's two year old child began to cry. She got up to take the child outside. The priest stopped his sermon and said, "Lady, Christ said for us to suffer the little children to come unto Him. You do not have to take the little child out of church, he doesn't bother me." The woman stopped, turned around and said smilingly, "But Father, you bother him." The whole congregation laughed. It livened up a dead sermon.

Humor takes the air out of high pressure stress tires. There is a lot of truth in the saying "smile and the whole world smiles with you."

A courageous sense of humor

You may have heard about the playful fellow who was exceeding the speed limit. A policeman pulled him over and walked up to him with his pen and ticket book in hand. The driver smiled and said, "I'll have a coke and two cheeseburgers." Fortunately the officer had a sense of humor and almost broke down laughing. He said, 'Slow down a little, but keep your sense of humor." The policeman smiled and added, "The guys at the station will never believe this!"

5. IS MY WORK SATISFYING?

```
|___|___|___|___|___|___|___|___|___|___|
0   1   2   3   4   5   6   7   8   9   10
```

When I was teaching in the school systems I often heard teachers say, "I'd quit, but I'm so high in the salary scale." They felt trapped, bored, and boxed in. They were in "golden handcuffs". Maybe you are in these same handcuffs with a boring job which you feel you can't change. Maybe your adult is not the chairman of "You, Inc." The average employee yearly spends 2,000 hours of precious life at his job. Boredom is a major cause of stress and 2,000 hours of boredom per year will take its toll.

Dennis Cyperyn, at the age of 35, chucked his partnership in a Detroit advertising agency and the $30,000 annual income that went with it. Today he paints signs for small food stores during the day, and plays a banjo with a local band at night . . . and he thoroughly enjoys it.

"U.S. News and World Report" (September 17, 1977) reports that for an increasing number of people, the good life means giving up a well-paying, high pressure job for work that is less boring and more satisfying.

Hans Seyle, the stress expert, contends that doing what you want to do is one of the most powerful stress reducers in life.

Recently, a friend of mine said, 'Jim, you better slow down or you'll have a heart attack." I said, "I collected more stress in one week working for a boss who thought he was God than in the three years I've been working for myself." If your job fits you and you are doing what you want to do, your job is a stress reducer. If your job boxes you in and is boring, you are in a stress producer. You may want to think about a change or you may never be around to collect the pension your job promised you.

6. IS MY WEIGHT WHERE I WANT IT TO BE?

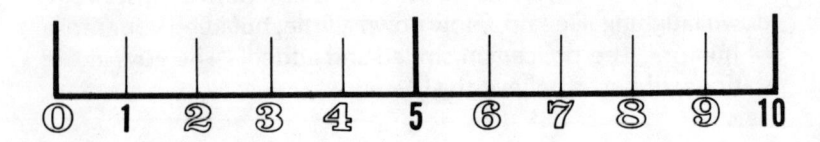

```
|___|___|___|___|___|___|___|___|___|___|
0   1   2   3   4   5   6   7   8   9   10
```

What does weight have to do with stress you may ask. Our research indicates that some people eat to cope with stress and that is where you get the foodaholic. This happened for a year and a half to a very dear friend of mine who said, "Jim, you can use my story for your book."

The story of Carol

Carol taught both of my little boys in kindergarten. Her latest relational stress proves the effect stress has on the human body. She told me the following story. "Fred and I were going together for over a year. We were even at the stage of picking a home in which to live. However, every time he went on a business trip I lost most of my excess weight. When he was in town I put on 15 to 20 pounds. Unconsciously I knew something was wrong with the relationship, but I did not have the courage to face it. Last month I found out that he still has a girl or two on the side. At last I faced the problem. I no longer have Fred but I have peace of mind as well as a healthy body. For a year and a half this stressful relationship has taken its toll."

Carol is back to tip-top shape and dropped off all of her excess weight. She did it by shutting down the relational stress generator, Fred. She gave up two forms of excess baggage: overweight and Fred.

Finding the hidden generator

Susanne, who lectures at weightwatchers, said that overeating is also often connected with a poor self-image. She said "I really didn't like myself when I was growing up. This causes tremendous stress. I ate to reduce stress. Once I ate two boxes of chocolates at one sitting. The heavier I got, the more I didn't like myself and the more I ate. It became a vicious circle. Learning to like myself shut down my stress generator."

Digging beneath to find the cause of overweight is definitely the way to go. Weight is just the symptom; some hidden generator is the cause.

Did you see the TV program "America, the Land of the Fats." They claimed that the average man is 30 lbs. overweight and the average woman 20 lbs. To top it off they claimed that only 6% of dieters persevere in order to lose weight. Maybe the goal of losing stress instead of losing weight is the better way to go.

7. CAN I GOOF AND GROW?

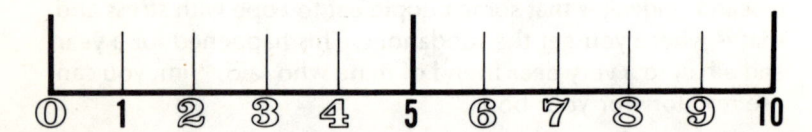

0 1 2 3 4 5 6 7 8 9 10

In doing research on stress, we found that one damaging parental edict which boxes many people in is perfectionism. The following are some telling statements. "You have to be the best or you'll let me down." (Notice the added "let ME down" guilt trip.) Another writes, "Be perfect, don't make mistakes." The assumption of "Be perfect, don't make mistakes" means that if you are human and make mistakes, you are not okay. Is it any wonder that so many Americans run around with a not okay feeling about themselves?

Here's a change. "Be human and goof and grow." To err is human. Making mistakes is a learning experience. So many kids learn to lie rather than admit a mistake because their parents are perfectionists and not humanists. This is also why so many "bosses" have the perfect Godlike complex.

On my refrigerator is a sign sent to me by a former student. It reads GOOF AND GROW. Just yesterday my little boy, Kenny, was floating his submarine in the bathtub. He said, "Dad, I took my submarine out of the bathtub and it had a lot of water in it and it spilled on the bathroom floor. Is that goof and grow?" I said, "Sure, pal, let's clean it up." If I had forced the "No Mistake" policy, he might have tried to blame it on his brother.

In working with people re-entering the single life, I've found this to be the cause of their greatest stress. That is why I called the last chapter of the re-entry book, "GOOF AND GROW".

If you feel lots of stress when you make a mistake, your parent is definitely the chairman of the board in your "You, Inc." Put your adult in charge so you can join the human race and goof and grow.

8. CAN I CONTROL FINANCIAL STRESS?

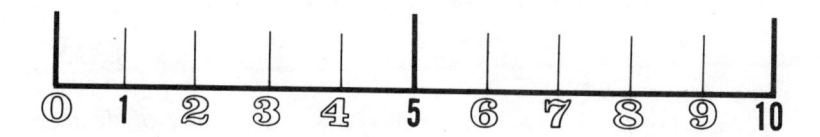

In our research we found that in every walk of life finances rank among the top four as a great cause of stress.

I had an uncle who grew up during the depression. He would have guilt feelings if he spent $2.00 for a movie. He never had a phone in his house because it cost money. He borrowed the neighbor's newspaper instead of getting his own to save money. He got money, but what was worse, money got him.

If your parent is chairman of the board, you may be like the fellow who wouldn't spend a dime to see an earthquake. If the child is chairman you may be bankrupt on a routine basis.

My uncle died and left all his money behind. Maybe he would have been better off if he were like the rich man who died some years ago and all of the relatives were on hand for the opening of the will. It read — "Being of sound mind, I spent all my money while I was alive."

This Christmas we visited a number of people. One fellow we know has more money than all my friends put together. In the spirit of Christmas we dropped in. What a barren and cold Christmas. They have four children who get no allowance; his wife is put on a strict budget. The children were seen but not heard during our short visit. We were not offered anything to drink, not even a glass of water or a cup of coffee. He has a lot of money; his family has loads of stress.

The same day we visited another family with four kids. We

were met with "Glad to see you," and "what would you like to drink?" Their children and their friends were in and out of the house, talking and laughing and having a good time. That Christmas we traveled from hell (the first family) to heaven (the second family). What was the difference? The first family was controlled **by** money and the second did the controlling.

Clearly we can trace this back to the philosophical generator of stress, namely that having (money) is much more important than being.

Today at lunch I met my old friend Ken Hornback. One of the things I admire about him is how beautifully he keeps money in perspective. Listen to his letter to his parents which I first published in my book **Re-entry Into the Single Life**, page 119.

October 8, 1976

Dear Mom and Dad,

Nobody likes to face the reality and inevitability of death, especially kids. You two, undoubtedly have thought about it and have a more mature attitude about it than I do so I am appealing for guidance from you about how I can face it too. You know I love you both very much. I have never had anyone close to me pass away and yet I know the day will come for you two, and for others I will know and love. So I want you to live knowing how very good and important I feel you are. We are quite different, it's true — over trivial matters like clothing, politics, economics, some beliefs, all stuff that changes. Over the basics, we are united — you are Mom and Dad, and I am Ken. I will always be thinking about you (especially when there is trouble — parents' major duties are as life-savers around the oceanside of life) so if you listen, wherever and whenever you are, you will feel me thinking.

I know you are dealing with estate and inheritance problems these days and you probably have some very sound ideas, financially. Feelings are a part of those decisions and I would like to express my feelings about your money and property; the finances are up to you. Please take my "share" and spend it on trips out to see me. Spend it now and often. My current life problems (and income) do not enable me to visit you as much as I want. I think my suggestion will make us both happy. Deliver the money after you die and it will be wasted because I will not be able to buy what I want — and need. Besides, if you spend it this way you can check out the expenditures and keep them low (ride budget air

fare, bring a bag lunch, etc.)
          Love,
          Ken

9. AM I A GOOD LISTENER?

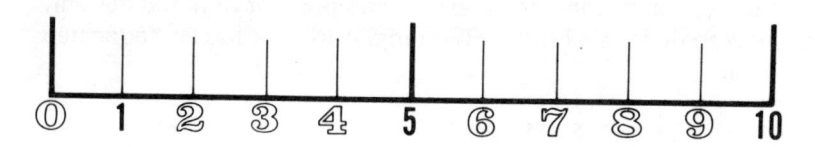

Until I was 37 years old, I was a good talker and joke teller, but a very poor listener. At 37, in a counseling technique course by Bill Sease, I learned the art of listening, the skill of getting into the feeling world of the other person. Since then, listening has been my hobby. Good listeners are those who can accept other people who have different values. Real listeners are candlelighters because they light the candles of worth and dignity in the people they listen to. Good listeners believe they can learn from anyone they meet. People who understand the feelings of other people and listen to them effectively reduce the stress in other people and increase growth in themselves. You learn from those you listen to.

After the first day of an effective listening class, a captain of detectives went home and listened to the values of his teenage son. The next day he came to class beaming and said, "Dammit, for 17 years all I gave were orders to my boy. Last night was the first time I ever listened to my son. What a neat kid I have! I never would have realized that if I hadn't listened to his values."

Of all the communication skills, none is more important than seeing things from the other person's point of view and the only way to do that is through listening. A listener has an "educated heart".

10. DO I HAVE A ZEST FOR LIVING?

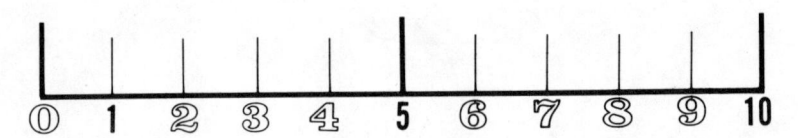

0 1 2 3 4 5 6 7 8 9 10

Recently I was giving a session on "stress reduction" at the elementary principals' conference. Fran and our two little boys came and we made a two-day vacation out of it. The first morning they were running around the exhibit area and they returned excitedly shouting, "Mom and Dad, come and see Donald Duck." We came and met Clyde, who was an exhibitor at the conference. He imitated Donald Duck perfectly and had spent time with our two boys. He showed them how to draw and gave them a blackboard. He has just as much zest for living as Kevin and Kenny.

Our two little boys with their zest for living found another little 43-year-old boy with a zest for living. Later "Donald Duck" came to our room for a drink before dinner. I will never forget what he said. "You know, Jim and Fran, I am a survivor of the school system. Your children are so free to be themselves. I was also, but I was punished for it. I had the record for suspension in my high school. Everytime I didn't conform, I was punished. The hardest thing I had to do was to finish school and keep my creativity." "Donald Duck" (Clyde) owns World Research Company, a construction company, and a toy company. He and his wife travel all over with their exhibits. He has a degree in art and is still developing his creativity. He is highly interested in marketing our books because he feels education needs to "have more fun and creativity". Having two "zest for living" boys who meet "zest for living" people certainly adds excitement and happiness to our lives. The evening ended with a laugh as our little boys asked if "Donald Duck" could babysit while we went out to dinner.

Donald Duck noted that in his opinion most principals at the conference had high stress and a low to medium zest for living. How do you rank and what goal could you create to increase your zest for living?

11. DO I LIVE THE PRESENT?

```
0  1  2  3  4  5  6  7  8  9  10
```

Probably one of the most successful personal growth organizations is Alcoholics Anonymous. They teach the alcoholic to live the present. The past is no longer here, the future does not exist. All we have is the ever present NOW. An old Irishman once said, "I lived a long time, worried about a hell-of-a lot of things, most of which have never come to pass." Learning to worry effectively can be done just by living the present and taking life as it comes — step by step, problem by problem.

Several weeks ago I was talking to a widow. Her husband had died ten years ago. Almost all of her conversation was about the past. She never dated, never went out with friends; she is still married to the past. Life is passing her by while she lives on her memories.

How would you rank yourself? What percent of you is married to the past? What percent to the future? Or do you live the present?

12. DO I EXPRESS MY FEELINGS?

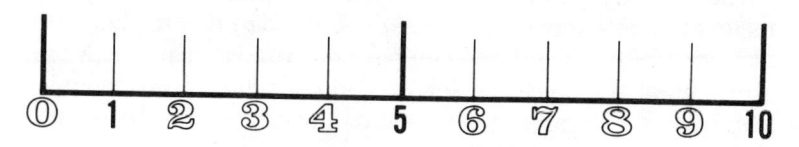

```
0  1  2  3  4  5  6  7  8  9  10
```

Repression of feelings was the hallmark of the days when I grew up. To a great extent it still is today by the glamorous "cool guy" on TV, the "big boys don't cry" or "emotions are a sign of weakness." It also could be pawned off as a religious virture, "Carry your cross and suffer in silence and your reward will be great in heaven." If any of the above edicts control your life, undoubtedly the parent part of your personality is chairman of the board . . . and your "You, Inc." is headed for disaster.

Repression of real feelings is a chief cause of stress which will either drive you crazy or put you in the grave. Expressing your feelings not only will keep you alive, but will help you to really know yourself, like yourself, and live life to the fullest.

The young woman's poetic words on feelings bear repeating.

For if you don't deal with the things that you feel
then you're only half alive and always reaching.
If you won't deal with all that you feel
You'll miss most of the lessons life is teaching.

If you don't deal with the things you feel, your "You, Inc." is only half alive.

You don't have to scream and shout to express your negative feelings. Here are two ways to express them non-verbally. You may want to try them. 1. I remember how I used to sit patiently in a restaurant waiting to be served and collecting stress. Now I learned in those cases to get up and walk out. I leave the stress with the waiter, waitress or the manager. My walking out is my way of saying, "I really don't like to be ignored." The moral of the story is - don't collect stress, express your feelings and you'll learn the lesson that life is teaching. 2. I was giving a workshop at Altus Air Force Base and a major showed me this stress reduction ticket he carries with him and it has done wonders for him.

I've rewritten the ticket using an adult-adult approach which will still release one's stress, but won't increase stress in the poor recipient of the ticket.

Citizen parking violation

This is not a ticket. When people park in two spaces I get angry and frustrated and feel like opening up a keg of nails and chewing the heads off. So I use this home made "ticket" to get my feelings out and also give you some feedback that you can use to change your behavior. There are a number of people like me who get irritated when one car takes two places. You probably are unaware of our feelings. Hopefully I have created an awareness that may serve as a help for you in future parking. I feel better because you know how guys like me feel and because I got it off my chest. I doubt that you did this to deliberately irritate me. Hopefully this feedback will be an incentive to leave parking room for guys like me.

With my compliments,
John Jones

13. DO I HAVE GOALS IN LIFE?

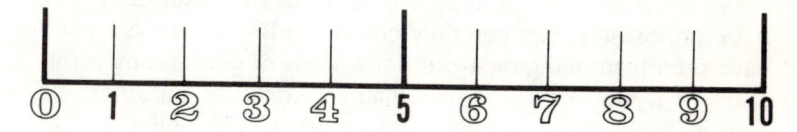

0 1 2 3 4 5 6 7 8 9 10

For 42 years my goals were like New Year's resolutions, always making them but never keeping them. Then Fran and I went to a goal setting workshop. We learned a simple but effective goal setting technique. For instance, we wanted to go out to dinner weekly but we never made it. We were told to list our obstacles to the goal. In this case it was a baby sitter. When we got home that evening our goal was to get a baby sitter. We went from house to house in the neighborhood and found one in a half an hour. Soon we were going out regularly to dinner and to talk. Since that time all kinds of things happened in my life through goal setting. I now have a seminar in goal setting and found that adding a reward is a big incentive for people. Annie and I just finished a seminar on goal setting for the Bureau of Standards. One young woman balked at rewards. "My dad used to bribe me with rewards to do what he wanted me to do." I said, "That is a whole different ball game. That is fulfilling someone else's oughts. In this case it is fulfilling your wants because you determine the reward." She liked that approach. The second day we shared rewards. Linda's goal was to lose 20 pounds and reward herself with a trip to Monte Carlo. Ruth's goal was to get her college degree and when she had accomplished this her reward would be a south sea cruise. Tom's goal was to get a management position and reward himself with a trip to the ancient ruins in Mexico. Your reward doesn't have to be that gigantic. I got myself a waterbed for losing 12 pounds. For a very few the achievement of the goal is reward enough. But for most, an attractive award is a dynamic incentive to reach the goal. It goes without saying, that once you reach your goal, you create another. A person without goals is a ship without a rudder.

Two months ago I was in Hawaii with John Roughan giving a mini-stress reduction workshop for a senior management seminar. I was on for one-half of a day and it was a three-day workshop. Most of the other sessions dealt with goal setting so I sat in on them. For several years I've been intrigued with the tremendous power of goal setting. I have shaken hands with millionaires and wealthy people who got where they are through goal setting.

My one point is that goal setting, without an awarenes of your basic philosophy, can certainly create loads of distress. What I have seen from hanging around the arena of goal setting is the reality that most of the goals are aimed at career and finances. That is "having and doing." Let's return to the philosophical generators of stress.

Figure A shows how most Americans set goals. (Unbalanced)

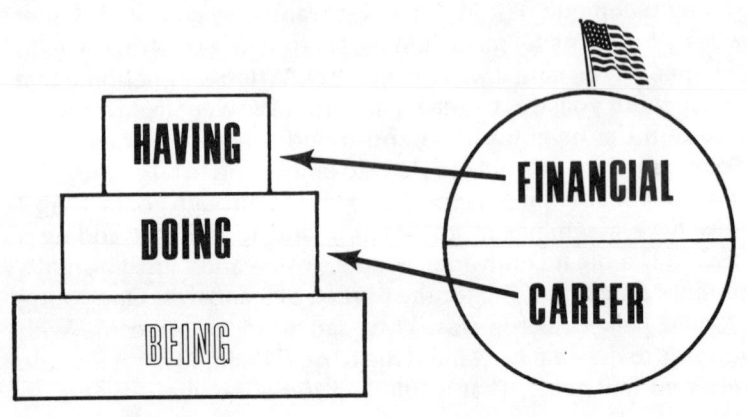

A.

Figure B shows the way they should be set for stress reduction. (Balanced)

B.

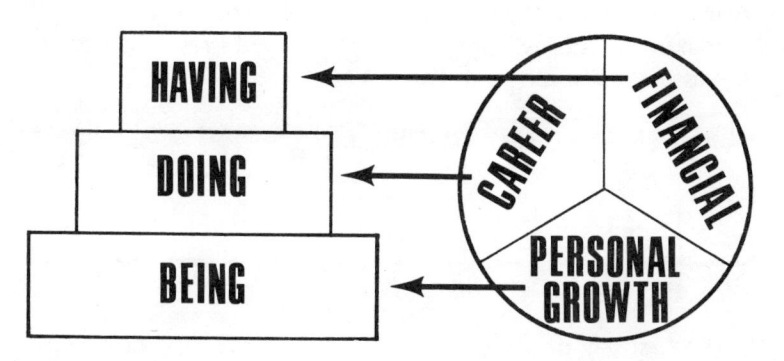

Unbalanced goal setting generates stress. Recently we had a small class for couples on communication in marriage. Every single family had "arrived". They had good jobs, a house in the suburbs, but they were literally empty in terms of communication. They were starving to death because they never set a goal that related to personal growth. I talked to two women who had three children each. One was on the verge of throwing in the towel on her marriage; the other was just at the frustrated stage. They loved the mini-seminar. They both said that this was the first time in their marriages they ever communicated on a significant level. My point is, they have reached their work goals, they have made their financial goals, but they are "married singles" because they have never set a "being" or personal growth goal. You may be wondering what some personal growth goals are. Here are some examples which those married couples could have added to their goals.

1. To take a course in communication or assertiveness training.
2. To have a special time daily to share feelings (not facts) about the ups and downs of a day, e.g., a daily feeling wheel.
3. To get away as a couple at least once a month.
4. To spend time (especially the fathers) listening to their children.
5. To plan taking a marriage encounter or similar workshop.

These are some personal growth goals. If all the goals are on "doing and having" and unfortunately they usually are, too often instead of happiness, they will create "married singles, and workaholics". The major cause of marriage breakdown is communication, not financial or career failure. Goals are phenomenal power tools. If they are aimed only in the direction of "doing and having" they could very well bring more distress than happiness. If they are aimed at "being, doing, and having" in that order, they will decrease the liability of stress and increase the assets of happiness in your "You, Inc".

14. DO I MANAGE MY TIME WELL?

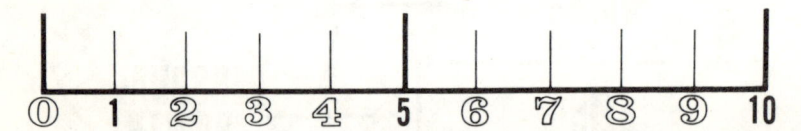

0 1 2 3 4 5 6 7 8 9 10

The first day of a secretaries' workshop in Dallas one of the participants said, "Jim, you ought to go to Six Flags. It is a good way to pass the time." My thought switched back to long ago when I was working as a stock boy for the Denver Dry. I did anything I could just to pass time. Now I value time so much, that I never look for something just to pass time. I feel that you only go around once and time is the most precious commodity of "You, Inc.". There are only 24 precious hours in a day. If you ranked yourself as a 2 or 3 on the time management scale, your "You, Inc." might well be wasting its most precious commodity.

Daily time management should flow from your major goals in life. An anonymous philosopher once said, "Yesterday is a cancelled check, tomorrow is a promissory note, and today is ready cash. Use it!!" You may decide that this is something you can incorporate into your "You, Inc."

Since today is ready cash, the first rule is "Do it now." Procrastination is a liability to your 'You, Inc." It creates stress and saps the vitality out of you. Next, make a time log of your day for seven days. This will be an eye opener. You may find a lot of time-wasting activities. They are like cancers. They drain off vitality. You have to apply radical surgery. Check your appointment calendar, your extra curricular activities, your reading list, your TV habits and ax everything that doesn't give you a feeling of accomplishment or satisfaction.

The next step is a big one. It is based on "accepting what we can't change," that is, most of us have more things to do than time to do it. Once we accept that, we reduce stress. The next step will reduce more stress. Make a list of the things to do each day. Now put an A after those things that are of supreme importance to be done. Put a B after those that are next in line of importance. Put a C after those things that you should get done, but can wait. Now the next step is vital. Spend your time on the A's first. They will cause you the most stress if you don't get them accomplished. A lot of people spend their time in the C's and end up with a lot of frustration and stress. Nancy found that her husband and son were in the A catagory. She expresses her A's in her poem.

Dear Jim,
   After taking your workshop and reading your book,
   It caused me to stop and take a good look.
   I looked in the mirror, and what did I see?
   I saw that I was not happy with me.
   I started to think of changes to make,
   What's really important, and what's just fake?
   I'm truly contented with the roles that I play,
   Yet, something is lacking from day to day.
   I have my teaching, which isn't a threat,
   But it's to my family, I owe my debt.
   I know I'm too busy most of the time,
   I need to equalize, and get into line.
   The things out of life I treasure so much,
   The love of my husband and son, as such!
   They're the ones who don't get their share,
   My schedule must change, I know where I care.
   The question's not now, "What shall I be?"
   I've decided today, "What's really me!"
   I love them the most, and I want to share,
   That's my real value! You brought it to bear.
        Many thanks,
        Nancy

By following these basic points you will be able to really decrease your liability of distress and increase your assets of satisfaction and achievement in your "You, Inc." If you are a professional time waster, it may mean your child is chairman of the board and your parent will be giving you guilt feelings. By applying these simple principles of time management, you will be putting your adult in as chairman of the board in the area of how your "You, Inc." spends its most precious commodity, TIME.

15. HOW WELL CAN I COPE WITH GUILT FEELINGS?

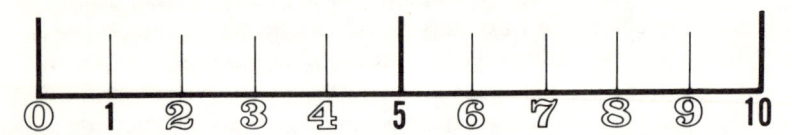

```
0   1   2   3   4   5   6   7   8   9   10
```

The day after Christmas Fran and I spent the day with our friends and their families. We got into a discussion about guilt feelings. Janice told us that she had very deep guilt feelings about working. After her last child was born she decided to go back to work three days a week, but she feels guilty because her mother says that good mothers ought to stay home with their children. Janice said, "I know that I am cranky, irritable, and hard to live with if I don't have my job, so I work and I feel guilty. I guess I fear that my kids may turn out wrong and then I will find out that my mother was right and will be coming over and saying 'I told you so'." I responded, "Your mother seems to want to live her life and also yours." "Right," she replied, "and she does it with little jabs regularly. For instance, she will say things like your children still need a security blanket. They wouldn't need one if you didn't work." After more discussion on how to handle guilt feelings, Sharon said, "Janice, my family was laying a guilt trip on me about the way Carl and I choose to live. I felt uneasy trying to talk to them about my feelings, so one day I sat down and typed them a six page letter. I took it over to them when they were all together, told them to read it and discuss it, and I left. Things really changed after that. Everybody got their feelings out and no more guilt trips about what we ought to be doing." Janice went home with a relevant New Year's resolution — "I'm going to write my mom a letter and take over as chairman of the board of "Me, Inc." I asked Sharon to write a synopsis of her letter. This is it.

Dear Mom & Karen,

I feel the time has come to clear the air. For weeks you've been taking jabs at Carl and me. You've let us know in no uncertain terms that you do not approve of the way we live our lives; that in your opinion we are making mistakes; and that our marriage is deteriorating. This letter is a feeling letter and I'm going to tell you our feelings.

We have been married for 19 years. In those years we had what most people would consider a good marriage. That may have been true then, but this is now. We want more. We don't choose to have a closed marriage any longer. We want it to blossom, to expand, and to grow in meaning. We love each other very much but there is room for more love, for a deeper understanding of love and life and that is what we are striving for. You feel that we are growing apart because we do not spend all our time together as we once did; because we've allowed other people into our lives; and because we've decided to be individuals as well as two people who are married. Because of this new freedom to be ourselves, we've found that the time we do spend together is more meaningful to us. It's a "want-to" in our lives instead of a habit or a duty. Our time alone is spent in meaningful talk and expressions instead of small talk. These are our values, our needs, and our lives. We are going to continue to live our lives exactly as we choose. If we do make mistakes or have problems, they will be ours, not yours. I know we are not wrong because when you grow as a person, you can never go backwards, only ahead. The mistakes you make help you, not hinder you.

We have always allowed all of you to live your lives as you choose and we have accepted your values. Is there some reason we cannot have that same acceptance from you? I will not let you treat me as a child any longer. If you can't accept us as we are then the closeness we all once shared is in grave danger. I want that closeness to remain and grow, but the choice is yours.
    Sharon

This letter actually freed Sharon from guilt feelings. Hopefully it will do the same for Janice.

Paralyzed by guilt feelings

Miriam told me the story of guilt feelings and their tremendous power. I asked her to put it in her letter and she did.

Kathy, the mother of three children, is a long term friend. She actually became paralyzed and appeared to have had a stroke or other serious ailment after the birth of her third child. The child was unplanned and unwanted by her but she repressed these feelings because she was a good Catholic with strong moral teaching; God will provide, etc. While in the hospital Kathy made a stressful decision to have her tubes tied to prevent another child. Kathy didn't want another unplanned child. After the operation she seemed fine until it was time for her to go home. She became paralyzed. Nerve specialists were brought in and after many days and many opinions, determined that she was suffering from psychosomatic disorder.

That was five years ago and now she is as normal as you and I... but, she spent almost a year of that time in physical therapy restoring her health.

Unfortunately there are loads of people boxed in by oughts imposed by others. The big question is do others make you feel guilty or do you "let" others make you feel guilty? Actually, when the adult takes over as chairman of "You, Inc." guilt feelings will disappear. I am not talking theory, but reality. It has happened to me and I have seen it happen to others... and it makes it all worth while.

16. DO I HAVE A SENSE OF BELONGING?

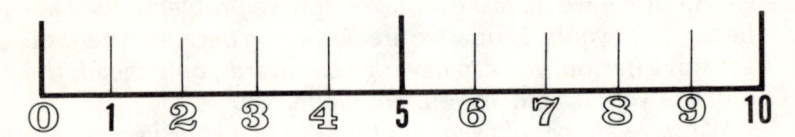

From time to time I hear someone, usually a man playing the role of the macho male, say, "I don't care whether other people like me. I say and do what I want to." If that were true, he just gave up a basic need for happiness. If we want to be happy, we have to care about other people liking us. We need to be loved, we need to belong.

If you ever lost your sense of belonging, your "You, Inc." would go into bankruptcy. In America, what happens to people who lose their sense of belonging is that they cash in their chips. Thousands of Americans commit suicide each year and more attempt it. Suicide among teenagers has increased 400% in the last five years. It is noteworthy to point out that individuals who are separated, divorced, or widowed are the greatest risks. Maybe they had all their eggs in one basket in the marriage and when the marriage went, their sense of belonging went with it. The rate of suicide among policemen is six times higher than the general population.

Suicide is rapidly rising among the young. A teacher in my class told me the story of her 24-year-old friend. He was living with Linda. He suddenly lost his job. The very next week, Linda decided to move out. He was panicked because he didn't know why she was leaving. Was it because of him, his job, what? He called her and asked her to come over for supper to talk it out. She never showed up. He had cooked a gourmet dinner and he was downcast. He didn't want the dinner to go to waste so he called every friend he knew to join him. They were all busy. He was all alone. He had lost his sense of belonging. He took a whole bottle of pills. Luckily someone found him in time. He was rushed to the hospital and he survived. To have a fulfilled life again, he will have to build up his sense of belonging.

Interestingly enough, Hans Seyle, whose research into stress is extensive, says, "One way to reduce stress is to earn thy neighbor's love." What he is saying is that we develop a sense of belonging by going out and working at it. Clearly, we have to "accept those things that we cannot change." One of them is your "You, Inc." needs to be loved. Listening, caring, and communicating are principal ways to "earn thy neighbor's love."

17. HOW WELL CAN I SAY NO?

We just finished talking about the need for a sense of belonging. Without this need we'll have tons of stress. However, as some fellow once said, "Everything in moderation." If we are overpowered by our need to belong, we will have a hard time being true to ourselves. As Shakespeare said, "To thine own self be true, and thou cannot be false to any man." When we can't say no to people, we will end up with too many irons in the fire, too much to do for others, no time to do the things we want. In other words, we will have a hell of a lot of stress, plus guilt feelings, because we were not true to ourselves.

You'll never know how many diets I've been on. I would be doing all right and then I'd be over at someone's house and they would say, "Have some more potatoes." I'd say, "No, I'm on a diet." They would say, "Hell, Jim, start it tomorrow." I would eat the potatoes. Then they would bring out the pie. I start my diet routine and they would say, "Well, you ate the potatoes... your diet is already broken, have the pie and start tomorrow." That went on for years. Then I learned assertiveness by teaching communication. I take my own classes and get in free. I've finally learned how to say "NO". Today I am 160 pounds, my ideal weight. I still meet people who want to lay some pie and ice cream on me, but I have learned how to take a stand for me. It is such a good feeling and has done so much for my "Me, Inc." that I would like to share it with you in hopes that you can use it in your "You, Inc."

First of all you have to answer the question. "Will others like me if I'm really myself?" I have a whole chapter on that in my first book, **Having Fun Being Yourself**, page 56, for those who want to go into more detail. The idea is very simple. It begins with you. You have to like yourself enough to be true to yourself. You want to be liked by others. The only way they can like you is when you are you. For instance, eating pie when I really wanted to keep my diet was not being me. I was playing the role of the accommodating fellow so people would like me. What I found out was that by being me and not taking the pie, I was still liked but they liked the real me. You really build wholesome relationships by being yourself. I have a motto which goes, "Most people will like you, some won't. You might as well be you, so you know who really likes you and who really don't." The motto is based on accepting things you cannot change. To assume that everybody will like you is not in line with reality. After all, Jesus Christ was extremely likeable, to say the least. Yet, not everyone liked him.

In fact, one of his best buddies Judas, turned him in. (Most people will like us, some won't, is accepting reality.)

One, two, three punch

Once you have made that part and parcel of your philosophy of your "You, Inc." you are now ready for the one, two, three punch that will actually set you free. You'll be able to say "No" without feeling guilty. Instead of guilt, you'll have the inner satisfaction of being true to yourself and building real relationships with other people.

STEP NO. 1 LISTEN

When someone asks something of you, take time to really understand what they are asking. For instance, Lois, a secretary whose boss's job was abolished, was asked by another secretary to help with some typing to beat a deadline. She really took time to understand the bind they were in. She said, "I really can understand the bind you are in due to the fact that Marge has been sick the last two weeks."

Once you step into their worlds and see the situation from their perceptions you have an adult-adult relationship. You are ready now for step 2.

STEP NO. 2 SHARING THE REAL "YOU, INC."

Lois had mixed feelings, so she shared them. She said, "Doris, my heart really goes out to you and I really would like to pitch in and help. Before my boss's job was abolished he gave me three weeks' work and right now I'm a couple of days behind. If I would try to help you I'd end up with too many irons in the fire and a lot of distress that I don't need."

STEP NO. 3 DO WHAT YOU REALLY FEEL

Lois concluded, "Sorry I can't help you, Doris, but I feel the best thing for me is to finish my two weeks' task. Maybe next time."

A friend of mine in government training said that using this 'one-two-three' approach for one year has really reduced stress and increased self-worth and peace in her life.

I can say the same thing. In fact, I now have reached the stage when it is enjoyable. In step one, I say, "I really appreciate the offer of pie and I know that the cook is happiest when the people eat the product." Then I move to step two and continue, "but I've really made a deal with myself (Me, Inc.) You know a couple of years ago according to my weight, I should have been 6'7". I decided that staying at 160 really gives me a good sense of accomplishment and that is important to me." Then comes Step No. 3, "So I'll pass on the pie." It is amazing how easy it is now, yet I never could do that for the first forty years of my life. At times I offer another solution, "Now if you really want to give the pie away, wrap it up and I'll take it home to my two little boys and they will take care of it."

Remember, "To thine own self be true" often means saying no to others but yes to yourself and in that way "You'll never be false to anyone."

18. DO I TAKE TIME FOR MYSELF

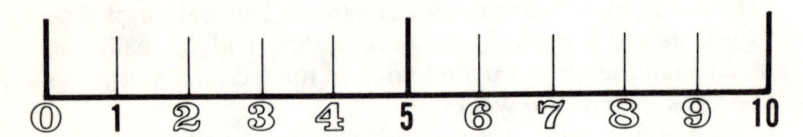

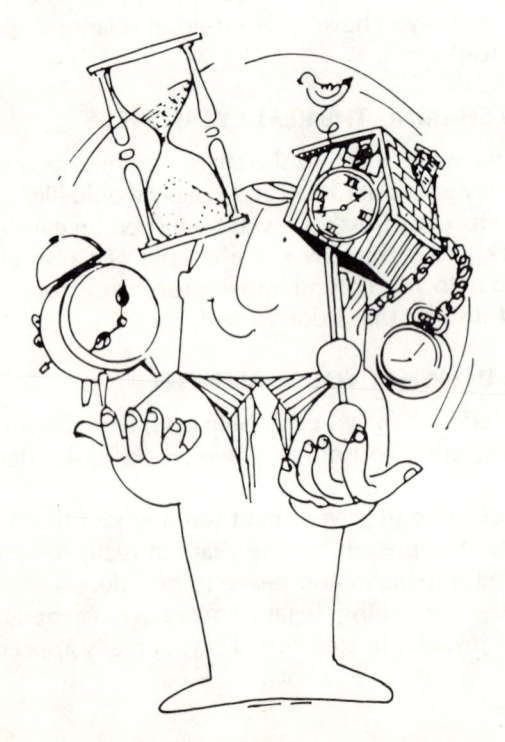

0 1 2 3 4 5 6 7 8 9 10

I can't help but think of the damage that the myth "It is selfish to do what you want to do" has done to so many people. We must take time out to accept the things that we cannot change. A changeless truth is, "we can't love anyone until we love ourselves." And yet so many feel guilty when they do anything for themselves. Dave made time for himself without shortchanging his family. He writes:

"I will get up one hour earlier than usual to have time for myself. I have a wife and two children and love them very much. I want to do their things and be with them, but I also have several things I want to do for me. When I do these things under my present schedule, I feel I shortchange my family. With this extra hour for me I feel a lot of problems and frustrations will be eliminated."

Often we are not aware of how little time we take for doing the things we want to do. Several months ago we did the time pie in class and Mary had three time pies. She was in the process of going through a separation. Her time pies were:

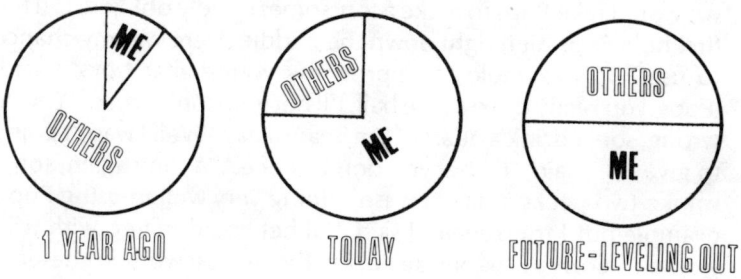

1 YEAR AGO — OTHERS (large), ME (small sliver)
TODAY — ME (large), OTHERS (small)
FUTURE - LEVELING OUT — ME / OTHERS (50-50)

She said she'll probably switch back to 50-50.

Then there is Lynette who spent 17 years taking care of four kids and fulfilling others needs. Today she works for a salary and has reduced some "oughts". She said, "I used to worry about the house; it had to be spic and span. Now I don't even make the beds anymore. If the kids want to make theirs - fine."

Then there is Lee, married for 19 years. She said that two years ago was the first decision she had made by herself in all those years. "I decided to return to school. When I got married, I went from my parents' house to my husband's house. It's really a thrill to begin to make room in my time pie for the things I want to do. I'm coming alive."

Being able to do what you want to do without feeling guilty implies that you are learning to love yourself. As one guy said, "You know, I think God did a good job with me. He gave me myself. If I learn to like myself, I am telling God thanks for the gift. If I don't like myself, I'm telling Him I don't think much of His gift."

Making room for things you want to do in life without infringing on the rights of others is a skill that will reduce the liability of stress in your "You, Inc." It brings you a sense of autonomy, achievement, and personal satisfaction.

19. DO I EXERCISE ON A REGULAR BASIS?

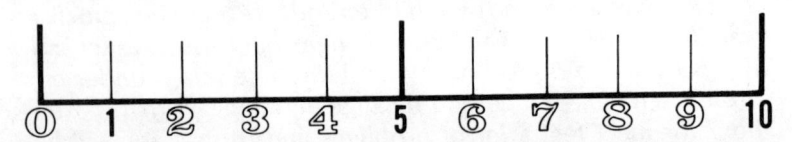

0 1 2 3 4 5 6 7 8 9 10

Fr. Jim Moynihan, my "free to be himself friend", exercises regularly on the golf course. He is 62 and looks like 16. If anyone has fun being himself it is Jim. The other day he said, "Jim, I gotta tell you this story. I took these two teenage altar boys golfing. It was real crowded. The 'pro' told me that he would let us tee off if we would take Pops to make a foursome. I gladly obliged. On the first hole Pops hit it right down the middle. Here was my chance to use Pop's example to impress my young altar boys. I said, 'Pops, you really drive a nice ball, I'll bet you don't drink.' 'You're wrong, son, I drink a quart of Jim Beam a day.' Well I wasn't going to give up. I said, 'I'll bet you don't smoke.' 'Wrong again, son, I smoke two packs a day.' I wasn't doing very well in using Pop's example but I tried again. I said, 'I'll bet you don't go with wild women.' 'Sorry ... wrong again, I'm the biggest women chaser in my neighborhood.' I finally leaned my golf bag against a tree and said, 'Pops, just how old are you?' He smiled, 'I'll be 29 tomorrow.' "

Pops had exercise but other things got to him. Exercise has two assets: it keeps the body tuned and it is an effective outlet for hidden stress.

The sleepwalker

Hidden stress reminds me of the story of the sleepwalker. During his sleepwalk he stabbed and killed the person in the neighboring apartment. Of course he wasn't aware of the deed, but the person is still dead. You may store stress in some hidden part of your unconscious, and some day "wake up dead" in your bed: You weren't aware of the stress, but you are still dead.

Researchers repeatedly point out that you can drink, eat fatty foods, do little or no exercise, and perhaps live into your seventies. Throw in the factor of stress, and you will never make it until seventy. So we are pushing exercise here in terms of a safety valve for hidden stress, as shown by the following studies.

1. University of Wisconsin researchers found exercise-induced chemical changes led to a definite decrease in anxiety levels.
2. Doctors at the University of Southern California reported a simple 15-minute walk was more relaxing than a strong tranquilizer.
3. A British medical team found as little as 10 minutes of suitable endurance exercise doubles the body's level of the hormone epinephrine (The chemical basis for happy feelings).

We have to find something that fits us. Golf for Bill is good exercise but for Bob, well, it "drives him crazy." Some kind of exercise that fits our "You, Inc." will reduce hidden stress.

Research in stress changed my life

My personal experience makes the point clearer. I was a jock when growing up but I never kept in regular condition since I quit playing football in 1947. After doing all this research in stress, distress, anxiety, and heart attacks, I found that researchers gave high marks to exercise as an outlet for distress and I significantly changed my life style.

I never bothered with exercise because I felt that I had reduced about 90% of the stress in my life by shutting down the generators. These were resigning from the priesthood in 1967; getting married and having children of my own (a fulfillment of a dream), becoming a counselor; resigning from the school system to work for myself; and mainly, forgetting about roles and concentrating on the fascinating search for "Who am I and what do I want to do with my life?" Actually, I saw myself having a high zest for living becase I'm 48 years old and still wondering what I am going to do when I grow up. That is a humorous statement but it contains a lot of truth. When searching for yourself is your major goal, you never arrive (unlike roles), you can never fully know yourself. Therefore, there is always adventure, excitement, and challenge in your life. Having all this going for me, I said, "Who needs exercise? I don't have any real distress to relieve." Several years ago I had one boss who was a psychopath who didn't have the decency to go crazy. I collected more stress in one week trying to work for him than I could have by working for myself for 50 years. Working for myself and trying to be myself was a dynamic combination that actually removed anxiety or distress from being a significant part of the scene in my life.

In reading the research on heart attacks, (finding exercise as a preventative and rehabilitative measure) I said to myself, "I am at one of the happiest phases of my life. I feel I am living life to the fullest. In fact, I don't even want a common cold, let alone a heart attack from hidden stress." As a result, for the last two years I've jogged regularly in the morning. I've lost 12 pounds and recently joined an exercise club where my two little boys and I have fun on the workout machine. We end up in the whirlpool. Kevin and Kenny lighten the atmosphere for other adult members because they bring their boats into the whirlpool and tell other adults, "You can play with our boats, too."

My research on stress and the heart brought out the importance of exercise. I have been in contact with Dr. Hank Brammell, a cardiologist who is the director of Rehabilitation Research & Training Center at the University of Colorado Medical Center. He put me through the treadmill test. I felt super because I checked out so well. Hank has some significant ideas which I would like to share with you.

He said that rhythmic or aeorbic type of exercise is the best for the heart. He does not recommend static or isometric because this type raises the blood pressure. He said that walking, jogging, cycling and swimming are where the action is in the field of exercising to keep the pump in prime condition.

Although he is competitive by nature he said, "I don't translate my competitiveness into running. I reach a level of fitness in a non-competitive style. I run four miles a day and it is also my thinking time."

I was impressed with his comprehensive approach to rehabilitation of coronary patients. He has two delightful assistants, Cidney and Judy. One is an occupational therapist, the other a physical therapist. They treat the whole patient, not just the heart. They assist the patients in coping with job stress, in learning exercise, and in time management skills.

He said, "Six years ago a 43 year old high geared Type A executive had a huge heart attack. As part of his program we helped him in four areas: 1. organize his time; 2. learn to say no; 3. go to out-of-town meetings a day early to relax and stay a day later; 4. refuse to take work home at night. Today, six years later, this person hasn't any indication of heart problems. So far we have a 90% return to work average."

Time was up. Hank had to go jogging. I said I would bring over a rough copy of this book in case he had some suggestions. I left his office with a feeling that **B.S. and Live Longer** is on the right wave length. In fact, I ended up with a good stress feeling of "I can't wait until this book is out."

The six - step stress reducer

If you just don't dig exercise, try this six-step approach relaxation response technique, described by Harvard cardiologist, Herbert Benson. In an article for the **Harvard Business Review,** "Your Innate Asset for Combating Stress," July, August, 1974, pp. 49-60, he states that you can do this between sandwiches at lunch. Many business executives use it, but don't wait until you become one to try it. Incorporate it into your "You, Inc." immediately.

Step 1. Sit in a comfortable position with your eyes closed; wear loose-fitting clothing.

Step 2. Relax your muscles, starting at the feet and working toward the head.

Step 3. As you inhale, mentally follow the air as it moves into your lungs.

Step 4. As you exhale, repeat to yourself some neutral word, such as "one" or a simple prayer of your own.

Step 5. Expect distracting thoughts. When they occur, merely say "Oh, well" to yourself and return to the repetition.

Step 6. Continue the exercise for 10 to 20 minutes. Do not use an alarm. When you finish, sit quietly with your eyes closed, then open them slowly before getting up.

20. HOW EFFECTIVELY DO I BREATHE?

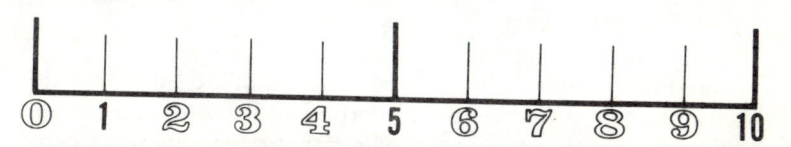

0 1 2 3 4 5 6 7 8 9 10

"What in the world does that have to do with qualities for coping with stress?" you are probably wondering. I don't blame you. Two years ago, after I strained my voice giving a workshop I had to take speech therapy to learn how to breathe. I also learned that most Americans are shallow breathers. From research in Yoga and Ikido I think the Eastern approach to stress has a lot to offer. For instance, if your breathing is choppy, rough, and short, you may find you have a high stress level.

Breathing is the most important among the various life functions. We can live for sometime without eating or drinking, but stop breathing and you'll find yourself at St. Peter's door. It is so basic. Food is broken down and burned to supply the energy needed to live. Oxygen is essential for this process. We get our oxygen through breathing. The average person's lung capacity is three or four thousand cubic centimeters, but in ordinary breathing he inhales only about five to seven hundred cubic centimeters of air. Using only a fraction of his capacity, his body food cannot be effectively turned into energy.

Learning how to breathe deeply we stimulate the exchange of oxygen and carbon dioxide and make ourselves powerful and fully alive.

Enough for the theory. Try it right now for five minutes or two (in case you are a super Type A and can't give five minutes). First, pin-point an imaginary point below your stomach and slowly pull in air through your nose, aiming at that point. When lungs are full hold your breath for a count of five. Now slowly exhale so that your breath travels infinitely to the ends of the universe. Close your eyes and relax while doing this and try to unify your mind and body. You may want to take a few minutes out of the day to reduce stress through this method. At the same time you'll be learning something you probably took for granted: the art of breathing.

21. HOW DO I RATE MYSELF IN TOUCHING?

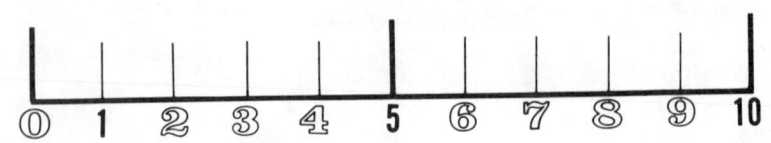

0 1 2 3 4 5 6 7 8 9 10

Some real thinker who crossed my path in life said, "We do well in the things we like to do." Perhaps that is why I am adding this quality. I rate myself as a 10 plus. If they had hugging percentiles like they do for I.Q.'s, I'd rank myself in the 99th percentile. It is my firm belief that everyone **needs** at least four good hugs a day. I always tell my class, "If you don't get v   I live at 7057 Wright Court."

In the following letter the names are ficticious but the letter is a real expression of the importance of touch to a wife whose husband is a non-toucher.

Dear Randy,

I don't know where to start writing this but I guess since we can't go anywhere without the kids, this is the only way I can get a few things off my chest.

Randy, as far as I'm concerned we really don't have a complete marriage any more. Days when you are at school I really look forward to your coming home. But usually you come in and don't even say Hi. I know that you had a terrible year, but deep inside I have too. Just once it would be nice to have a kiss when you get home or just to **be touched** once in awhile. Have I gotten so bad to look at that you can't stand to look at me in the daytime? Do you realize that the **only** time you touch me is when we are in bed and you want or need to make love (two or three times a month), maybe.

Susan has asked me several times why you can never show any affection. They are always holding hands or touching each other like they enjoy being together and in love. Any time I try to wrap my arms around you or hold hands you push me away like I've got the plague. I guess it's like father like son. I don't remember ever seeing your dad touch your mom.

Last year I was really looking forward to our tenth anniversary. I really thought it would be something special. The dinner was fine, but not once during the day or night did you even touch me or say that you loved me.

Randy, I love my home, you, and the kids; but a home has to be more than a place to eat and sleep.

Maria

The letter speaks for itself about the power of touching.

A lesson from research

Research with monkeys is striking. One group experienced regular touching from their mothers. The other group were fed, but not touched. They died! In an orphange in South America infants were given everything essential to their biological needs, but were never picked up and cuddled. They curled up and died. Touch is not a fringe benefit. We need it. I love the bumper sticker DID YOU HUG YOUR CHILD TODAY?

Meaningful touch

I have to qualify touching. Lots of people have sex, but they are not thoroughbred touchers. I remember my high school classmate telling me about his episode. He went to the drive-in movie with Lori. He was into some heavy necking. After awhile he said, "Lori, do you want to go in the back seat?" She said, "No." Awhile later he tried again and got a firm "NO". After more deep passionate necking, he finally said, "Dammit, Lori, why don't you want to go in the back seat?" She innocently replied, "Chuck I'd rather stay up here with you."

By the way, Chuck was not a toucher. He was going through the "one night stands" and the necking scene that was and still is a part of teenage life. Unfortunately young people often confuse "hot pants" with meaningful touching. Maybe that is why so many huggers marry non-huggers. As Betty said, "I thought my husband was a hugger when we were going together, but since we've been married, he never touches me except once a week in the bedroom and then it's 'bam, bam, thank you ma'am.' "

The power of touch

Several years ago we had a goal setting workshop. Marilyn was having trouble in her marriage. She was about to throw in the towel, but felt she should make one last try. She felt that she was totally a "married single" because her husband grew up conditioned to the old eternal law that "it is a weakness for a man to express his feelings." After exploring ways to bridge the gap, she decided on the non-verbal method of simple but regular touching. She would simply rest her hand on his knee while watching TV or pat him on the shoulder and say, "Did you have a nice day?" I asked her to report on the endeavor. A month later I received a beautiful letter which I would insert here, but I mislaid it. In essence she said, "I'm staying married. The simple touching has built a bridge of warmth and comunication I've never experienced in 18 years of marriage."

Touching as a supervisor

Recently we were giving a workshop in Salt Lake and had coffee with Linda, a real good friend of mine. She was sharing the stress involved in working for a boss who could have played the lead robot in Star Wars. She told me that he sees his role of supervisor as "a huge battleship with thick iron sides which the roughest waves cannot penetrate." Some day he may find out that his body is not a battleship, and he will sink into intensive care in the cardiac ward. In the meantime, she is under super high stress trying to communicate with a battleship.

I can't help but compare this battleship with another government supervisor, Kurt. He is always patting people on the shoulder and radiating warmth and acceptance. The distress between the touching supervisor and the battleship is as different as night and day.

If you are a non-hugger, remember it is a learnable skill. Learn it gradually; try it on little children, they love it and need it. Expressing feelings through the world of touch will give you a new dimension in life.

Touch in marriage

My good friend Mary took a class on assertiveness training. She and her husband dropped over for coffee one evening and I said, "Well, what did you learn today?" She was all bubbly and smiles as she reported that her teacher had said that Americans lack sexual assertiveness because so many still have anxiety in talking about sex. Our teacher told us about a super-neat experiment that I think we should discuss. She told us to go somewhere with your spouse to a place where you can be totally alone, preferably with a fireplace. Take along a bottle of wine, baby oil, anything else you want to for a beautiful night or weekend. This is a touching experiment; it's done in three phases. It can all be done in one night or spread out over the weekend. First of all get the setting ready, the fire going, the wine poured, the towels or blankets down in front of the fireplace, the baby oil handy, and of course you must be nude. The first step is to touch, rub, talk, ask questions, anything that will let you know what the other person feels, wants, desires, etc. You must only touch those parts of each others bodies which are not considered private (in old fashioned terms). You can do this one at a time or together, whatever fits you. Take your time when doing this, time to discover all the hidden secrets about the human body. Now you go one step further, touching all parts of the body. This also should be done very slowly and with a lot of expression and don't forget to tell each other what feels good and what doesn't. The third step is of course making love. By this time you should know enough about your partner's body, his likes and dislikes, his wishes and desires, to have a really neat experience; one that will be very fulfilling to you both."

Touch is a vital tool of "You, Inc." It is a beautiful development of the child member of the board of "You, Inc." By and large, the child part of our personalities has been boxed in and underdeveloped. Consider seriously letting your child grow through the power of touching. "Indeed," as my friend, J. Brady said, "experience the power of touch and it will set you free."

That's all there is

I can't help but think of the old song, "That's all there is, there ain't no more, St. Peter said as he closed the door." We have just closed the door on a general audit of your "You, Inc." From our audit on stress, it is overwhelmingly clear that the key to beating stress lies with YOU.

Faye, in her life, used this key. She was unique, different, but surrounded with the stress of "what will others think?" She finally accepted **those things she could not change**, namely what will others think, and she began working on **those things she could change**, namely herself.

She put it all together in a powerful poem (**RE-ENTRY INTO THE SINGLE LIFE,** p. 111).

Faye hits the nail on the head

The big learning experience of re-entry has to be the switch from role to identity. Last summer, a serene and quiet woman was in my class. She did a fabulous job of capturing this message of "being yourself" in the following poem.

Will others like me if I'm really myself?
That's always caused some concern you see.
I don't play all my expected roles too well.
I have to find some time to be free
From social commands and job's demands.
I need a lot of time to be me.

I don't like baby showers and ladies luncheons
Or chit-chat over a cup of tea.
Because I'm a woman I'm supposed to go.

Don't I know that's my social duty?
I have often said "no" when I wanted,
But then I would begin to feel guilty.

I don't invite people to my house for dinner.
There's a pool table where the dining should be.
You can show off your latest new dessert,
But I will never ask for the recipe.
I must reciprocate because that's the rule.
What restaurant would you like to see?

Society says "selfish" you don't have children.
You can't mean that you don't want any.
Though some ladies had them without a thought,
Then decided to ignore them miserably.

*They all encourage others to do the same,
When though they sometimes suffer mentally.*

*I much prefer to do what I like
Than to attend the loveliest party.
It's not that I don't like people.
It's the small talk that gets to me.
That's why all parties should be "happenings",
Being quiet without being thought crazy.*

*I don't play my expected roles too well.
I have to have time to be free.
It's caused me some concern that I haven't conformed
To what a sociable woman is supposed to be.
But now that I've taken this class of yours,
I'll say, "Tough shit — THAT'S ME!"*

A tune-up or overhaul

The "do, do, do" or "go, go, go" type A people are easy targets for the "five easy ways to reduce stress" approach, which is so widespread. Faye, in her poem, exemplified the effective "overhaul" approach instead of the superficial "tune-up" approach. She overhauled her whole view of the "oughts and shoulds" of others. In so doing she practically shut down a stress generator in her life.

Remember the story of the caterpillars trying to get to the top of the mountain and knocking each other down to reach the top? One caterpillar got out of the type A "rat-race" of the caterpillars and overhauled his approach. He became a butterfly and began flying freely all over from flower to flower. He had time to "stop and smell the roses".

Helping you transform yourself from a caterpillar to a butterfly is a major goal of this book. To make it a reality, take a look at yourself (You, Inc.), the one thing you can change. From the 21 areas on which you just ranked yourself, pick one in which you feel you need improvement. Set a specific goal to make a change. In doing this you have taken the first step in overhauling a major stress generator "Yourself". Be sure to carry our recommended tool with you:

"Lord, give me the serenity to accept those things I cannot change . . . the courage to change the things I can (i.e. myself) . . . and the wisdom to know the difference."

Do this and I'll "betcha" that you'll **Beat Stress and Live LONGER.**

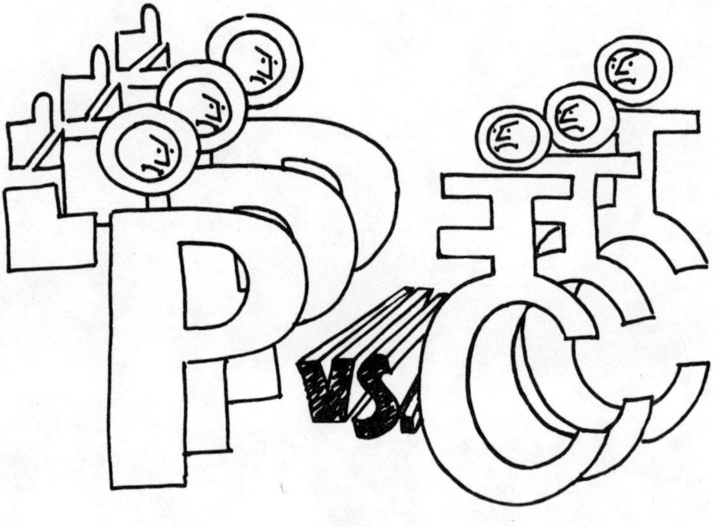
P vs C

APPENDIX

HOW CAN YOU REDUCE STRESS IN STUDENTS AND CHILDREN?

Last year on our way home from a university class of teachers, Annie was interestedly reading the results of their surveys. She looked up and said, "Jim, I just got a brilliant idea. We should adapt this survey for kids." Immediately she became the chairperson and in a few weeks data began flowing in. The survey turned up their major stress points. It was relational stress, e.g., parents, teachers, brothers, and sisters. Boredom was high on the elementary level; money was high on the secondary level. What is really interesting is that children put adults (parents and teachers) in the top three in their survey, and adults put children in the top three of their survey. They could start a "Mutual Stress Society."

Fearless Freddie

"Fearless Freddie" runs the management seminars for the Denver Civil Service Training Commission. He is, perhaps the best trainer I've come across in the government. Last week Annie was telling him about how teachers ranked on top of the list in the student stress surveys. He said, "I know what you mean. For three years in grade school, all I heard was, 'Wait until you get Miss Chambers.' I finally got her. The first day she was writing the assignment on the board. Sam, who sat across from me, laughed. She snapped, 'What was that for, Samuel?' He said, 'I saw your garter.' 'Take your books and don't return for three days,' she yelled. When she resumed writing, Bill hee-hawed. 'And what caused that, young man?' she shouted. 'I saw both of your garters,' he bashfully replied. 'Take your books and don't come back for a week,' she snapped. Obviously upset by this rebellious eighth grade, she dropped the chalk and bent over to pick it up. I got my books and headed for the door. 'Where do you think you are going, Frederick?' she barked. 'From what I saw, Miss Chambers, my school days are over.' Since that day I got the name of 'Fearless Freddie'."

You can't give what you don't have

This philosophical gem fits stress to a "T". If you don't have stress, you won't give any to your children or students. Any experienced counselor will tell you that uptight parents create uptight children and uptight teachers create uptight students. Collect stamps, coins, or green stamps, but don't collect stress because "you can't give what you don't have."

Measuring stress levels

Here is a simple little test that you can use to measure your stress. (Adapted from "Stress and How to Cope with It," John Farguhar, **the Stanford Magazine,** Fall/Winter, 1977) You probably will want to take it yourself. If you rank high, you may want to take steps to reduce your stress. By doing this, you will automatically reduce the stress of your children, your students, and all with whom you come in contact.

WHERE OH WHERE CAN MY STRESS LEVEL BE?

	OFTEN	A few times a week	RARELY
1. People at work, home (or school) create tension in me.	2	1	0
2. I'm tense, anxious, or have a nervous stomach.	2	1	0
3. I take tranquilizers, drugs (or marijuana) to relax.	2	1	0
4. My day is made up of many deadlines.	2	1	0
5. It is hard for me to concentrate on what I am doing because I am worrying about other things.	2	1	0
6. I can hardly find time to relax.	2	1	0
7. Even when I have time, I find it hard to relax.	2	1	0
8. I can't turn off my thoughts at nights or weekends long enough to feel refreshed the next day.	2	1	0
9. I have migraine or tension headaches, pain in my neck or shoulder, or I don't really get much sleep at night.	2	1	0
10. I smoke, drink, or eat when I get uptight (or to reduce stress).	2	1	0

ZONE
1. 14-20 Considerably above average.
2. 10-13 Above average.
3. 6-9 Average
4. 3-5 Below average
5. 0-2 Considerably below average

Unless you are in zone five, you have something to work on in stress management. Incidentally, using tools to more effectively relate to children will reduce stress in you as well as in them.

The major tool with children

Jack, an assistant principal, wrote in a letter, "I have a slogan which I have shared with teachers often. It goes like this: I CARE NOT HOW MUCH YOU KNOW, UNTIL I KNOW HOW MUCH YOU CARE." In that saying lies the greatest tool of stress reduction for children. The following ways are probably the most effective stress reducers that I've come across. For the sake of clarity let's go back to "You, Inc." You have three people on your board. So does each child. Using that model, we will classify the following approaches to stress reduction under them. Choosing the most effective model to communicate with children is making your caring come alive.

1. Critical parent-child (what not to do)
2. Nurturing parent-child
3. Adult-adult
4. Child-child

I. Critical parent-child approach

I heard a cute saying the other day — "Insanity is inherited, we get it from our children." There is a lot of truth in that; however, parents and often teachers like Miss Chambers help to drive children nuts. That's why the wise old philosopher said a mouthful when he wrote, "Children should be highly selective when choosing their parents."

An expert in family relations did a study on how Americans parent their children. Here's what he found.

A. Moralizing . . . "When I was your age we were lucky to have anything to eat."

B. Commanding . . . "As long as you live here, you will follow my rules."

C. Interpreting . . . "Now Johnny, you really don't hate your friend."

D. Diverting . . . "Now just have something to eat and forget all about it."

E. Ignoring . . . "Don't bother me, talk to your father."

F. Advising . . . "You should be a good girl and not talk back to adults."

G. Threatening . . . "If you don't do it now, I'll ground you for a month."

All of these can be catagorized into a parent-child relationship. Unfortunately it is the "critical parent" which creates distress, anxiety, and a not-okay feeling. We are appalled at the number of physical child abuse cases and we are just becoming aware of the more widespread mental or "self-image" child abuse.

Remember the killer statements of managers who create stress in their employees? Perhaps they learned them from their parents. Here are quotes collected from parents and teachers.

Killer statements

1) "You idiot."
2) "You're a klutz."
3) "Your brother did so well and you are going to be the family dumb-bell."
4) "You shut up until you are spoken to."
5) "Don't you ever raise your voice to me again."
6) "Why did I ever have children?"
7) "My God, you've done it again."
8) "What will the neighbors say?"
9) "Can't you pay attention?"

10) "Where were you when God passed out brains?"
11) "And I tried my best to raise you as a good boy."
12) "How could you do that to your mother?"
13) "You are the laziest thing in God's creation."
14) "Keep that up and you'll end up as a bum."
15) "You'll never amount to anything."
16) "What a knuckle-head."

A discipline that kills the positive self-image

Killer statements often hide under the name of discipline. Discipline comes from the Latin word "to teach" and not "to put down". Killer statements also many times produce shyness and kill the "okay" feeling in kids. I cringe when I hear people say to other parents, "You have such nice children, they are so quiet." Fortunately, we had open communication in my home. But I grew up when "good children were seen and not heard." The message was, "don't talk until you're 21." Then you hear, "He's 21 and so quiet." Well, of course, he had no practice . . . what do you expect?

Recently, a government secretary in Salt Lake put in a personal pitch against critical parent-child approaches when she said, "My little four year old talked back to his baby sitter. I yelled back at him, "If I ever hear you speaking up to adults again, I'll really spank you!" Almost with tears in her eyes she said, "He has not spoken to adults for four years. We've been going to counselors for the last four years. I hope he comes out of it." This is clearly a critical parent-child relationship which creates stress instead of reducing it.

Creators of ulcers, suicides, and shyness

The critical parent-child approach is producing ulcers in elementary school children. Research is turning up more and more cases of ulcers among those children. Japan's educational system has high pressure to produce and they are finding suicides among elementary school children. In 1977, more than 700 children and teenagers took their lives in Japan.

Japanese authorities offer two reasons for this suicide rate: 1. the country has a fiercely competitive educational system in which the road to success in later life is linked to passing difficult entrance examinations to leading universities; 2. children react negatively to the mounting pressures of excessively regulated lives.

Philip Zimbardo claims that in America our problem is not lack of discipline but lack of assertiveness. He feels that shyness has reached epidemic proportions. He expresses his ideas very well in his book entitled **Shyness**.

For five years, Zimbardo and his colleagues studied shyness in the United States and other countries ... interviewing over 5,000 adults. They concluded that shyness is mostly a cultural phenomenon. In Japan, shyness is instilled in the children as a means of total control; the choice is "learn to be inhibited or pay the price of rejection." In Israel, however, "Chutzpah" is valued and every success is praised, while failures are noted and allowed to pass. In the United States there is a little of each. We don't give children as much credit for successes as we should — although it's not the complete denial of praise you find in Japan. But, we are hard on them for failure. We say, "Look how bright your brother is," or "how bright the neighbor is." We make our love contingent on performance. Imagine the amount of stress that could be avoided if parents and teachers ever adopted the goof and grow philosophy and let children use mistakes as a means of learning. In a recent speech on shyness, Zimbardo said, "I get so depressed sitting in elementary school classes day after day and seeing these kids who are nearly autistic. Their lips move but they never sing out. These teachers pride themselves on their tight classroom control. Unfortunately they are creating shyness — the fear of asserting oneself in relationships with others. This is by far a greater problem than a lack of discipline."

The other side of the coin

Two stressful sides make up the critical parent-child coin. It creates stress in students and children, and they are reducing it by "getting even" with their teachers or parents.

In 1976, 6,000 parents went to court in Maryland alone to give up their responsibility for their teenage children. They could not cope with the stress caused by the "let's get even" attitude of their children.

Teacher - student war

1. Since 1961, the number of teachers with 20 years or more experience has dropped by half, most of that decline being in the

last five years.

2. Students are starting a war with their teachers to reduce their stress.

3. It is estimated that 70,000 public school teachers will be physically assaulted in their classrooms. (Only ten percent report it.)

4. Eighty percent of Los Angeles' inner-city school teachers are on Valium.

5. Milwaukee schools have set up a hospital program to treat alchoholism in teachers.

6. In a survey on "Is Teaching Hazardous to Your Health?" most of the 10,000 teachers cited stress as their biggest health problem. They complained of headaches, hypertension, and nervous stomachs.

7. A Senate subcommittee to investigate junvenile delinquency reported last year that school violence had become so common that the only difference between "tough" city schools and those in the suburbs was one of degree. In a three year period attacks on teachers were up 80%, assaults on students up 85%. Senator Birch Bayh (D., Ind.) the subcommittee chairman, warned, "For a growing number of students and teachers the primary task is no longer education, but preservation."

8. Since 1971, Dr. Alfred Bloch, a Los Angeles psychiatrist, has treated over 600 teachers for what he calls a new form of combat neurosis.

"They suffer from the same wartime psychological symptoms, emotional tension, anxiety, insecurity, nightmares, blurred vision, dizziness, fatigue and irritability. Their physical symptoms are also similar — ranging from headaches and skin disorders to peptic ulcers, hypertension and respiratory problems."

"Fear," the psychiatrist said, "is the most potent source of the stress. Teachers fear the students, administrators who will not give them support, and the elected school board who cannot or will not provide them with adequate protection because of budgetary problems. They fear coming to work, they fear leaving work, and they spend their entire workday in a state of anxiety." (From "Our Nation's Teachers Are Taking A Beating", **Rocky Mountain News,** 1978, by Marguerite Michaels.)

This could all be summed up by the new "Three R's". Rest, rotation, and recuperation from combat zones have to be given many teachers at the end of a two or three year period.

Is there a message?

The message of Martin Luther King and the civil rights movement was that blacks were tired of the critical parent-child role that society had laid upon them. The Women's Liberation movement is saying that they are tired of that same parent-child role and they want equality. These kids, I believe, are saying the same thing by starting the student-teacher war.

The fear-stress chain

After reading the statistics on the revolt of the students of today, you may share the reaction of one woman who said, "What is wrong with today's children?" People immediately assume that the kids are in the wrong. It is really a hang-over from my days when the teacher was always right. Recently, one high school girl from Chicago said, "As students, we have no rights. We do something wrong, we are sent to the office. Our parents are called. If the teacher is neurotic, psychotic, or just wrong, we have to grin and bear it. Teachers have tenure. They have to shoot a student before they are liable for dismissal." Many educators agree that the students need a bill of rights. Did you ever hear of a student sending a teacher to the office or calling the parents of the teacher?

Let's look further. Behind the scenes (and I have been behind them) there is the hidden stress generator of fear. Here is how it works. The board of education often puts the superintendent in the role of the child. The superintendent, in turn, acts out of his critical parent and puts the principals in the child role. The principals turn around and create a critical parent-child role with their teachers which creates stress in them. The teachers get rid of their stress by giving it to the student in the same parent-child communique. The students are left holding the bag of stress. Some become the shy adapted child. Others go home and kick the dog. Some, however, are rebelling and tossing the stress right back to the teachers. This fact, perhaps more than anything else, is the basic cause of the teacher-student war of today.

The old line, "These kids are not like the kids in our day," is true. In our day we had no choice but to tolerate the critical parent-child role in schools. Today, the students are revolting. Their means may be wrong, but their message seems valid. They are tired of being the stress collectors from the educational "fear-stress chain." If we want to end the student-teacher war (and the parent-children war), we will have to attack and curtail or shut down the powerful stress producing generator of critical parent-child communication which now permeates most of our educational systems as well as our home environments.

Parent-child approach hits big students also

Teachers are also students. Many refuse to go through a higher degree program because, "In no way is it worth the hassle." Translate "hassle" and you will come up with critical parent-child relationships. Let's look at some real examples.

My neighbor, Annette, returned to school after 17 years. Last week she came over for a drink to reduce her stress. "I can't believe it," she said. "Our accounting teacher treats us like two-year olds. After ordering us not to write in our workbooks, she told us to hold them up. Rudy had filled in the first line. The teacher went into orbit yelling and screaming. I could not believe it. In my next class, Little Napoleon walked in in disguise. He spent the whole first class explaining his rules which you keep or flunk. Thank God, the teacher in the last class was a human being who treated us as adults."

Mitch was my good friend in graduate school. The dean arbitrarily discounted two credits from another university on the basis that, "they don't teach it like we do." Mitch made an appointment to talk it over. There was no talking except, "Take it or go elsewhere."

A year ago I had an outspoken principal in my class. When discussing parent-child communication, he said, "I've been boxed in by my bosses for 24 years. Most of them lived in fear of what others would think . . . the parents, the administration, or the board of education. No one seemed to care about what the students thought. When I retire I am going to write a book entitled **The Sons of Bitches and Bastards in Education.** The rest of the class spontaneously clapped.

During class I was talking to a teacher with a high stress level. She showed me her evaluation given by her vice principal on Feb. 8, 1978. I asked for a copy. Put yourself in her shoes as you read this stress-producing critical parent-child communication.

I have the following concerns or recommendations that we need to discuss:

1. I want to see a plan developed by you for a minimum of three

groups in math. I can see no reason why all students are doing the same assignment. You need to provide for individual differences. This plan is due in my office by Monday, February 13, 1978.

2. The textbooks behind your file cabinet next to your desk will be brought to the office by no later than Friday, February 10, 1978. County policy states that all books with a copyright of 1967 or earlier will be disposed of.

The phrase "that we need to discuss" implies an adult-adult relationship. The real meaning is "come in and I will **tell** you what to do!"

I felt empathy for this stress-filled teacher caused by an "I'm okay, you're not okay" principal. It may be some consolation for her to know that others are worse off. For instance, Ms. R. is a Los Angeles teacher who had her hair set on fire. She put out the blaze herself and ran to tell the principal. Instead of receiving help, she was criticized for leaving the classroom. She was also instructed not to discuss the assault with fellow teachers. She continued teaching but slowly dropped into severe depression. Finally, she attempted suicide. Despite therapy, she has been unable to return to the classroom.

These are real people, real stories, and real stresses. John Roughan and I were discussing this area at lunch. He made a relevant comparison. He lived in Guadacanal for 17 years and is returning when he finishes his proposal. He said, "Developing nations often find themselves in a parent-child relationship. Rarely are they consulted. They are told what is good for them. If they don't go along they are threatened with withdrawal of funds, just as some teachers use flunking as a threat." We ended up agreeing with the axiom "power corrupts and absolute power corrupts absolutely in a number of cases." When it does corrupt, you end up with a critical parent-child relationship.

Parent-child situations are generators of stress in all areas of life. If there is ever to be a change, what better place to start than the home and the school.

There is a bright side to the picture. For instance, programs like Parent Effectiveness Training are cropping up all over to help parents communicate more effectviely with their children. There are thousands of humanistic teachers and administrators who are trying to humanize education by replacing the critical parent-child relationship with an adult-adult or I'm okay — you're okay relationship.

I personally have attended seven colleges and universities. The

University of Northern Colorado in my perception is a leader in humanizing education. I spent two years in their college of education and am extremely impressed with the number of professors who communicate on an adult-adult with their students. Fortunately, they train teachers; as a result they have a tremendous impact in the school systems.

II. Nurturing parent - child approach

The nurturing parent creates the warm fuzzies that everyone, especially little kids, need to learn to develop the feeling that they are loved and wanted. Take away that feeling and you have stress of the highest order. There are many ways to give warm fuzzies, e.g., hugging, a smile, a wink, a little note of thanks, a happy gram which some teachers send home to parents complimenting the child's behavior.

To make verbal warm fuzzies reduce stress, two things should be kept in mind. Compliment the activity and not the person. If you say, "Now that is being a good girl," you may give the child stress. This was brought out to me by a teenager when I was a school counselor. "My parents really bug me. They keep telling me I'm a good girl. To me that means that they want me to be just like them. I want to be myself." Aim your warm fuzzies at their

33 ways to give Warm Fuzzies

1. I LOVE YOUR TIE.
2. THANKS FOR CUTTING THE GRASS.
3. YOU SURE CATCH ON FAST.
4. THAT IS A NICE DIVE.
5. YOU REALLY CAN HIT THE BALL.
6. THANKS FOR CUTTING ME IN ON DECISION MAKING.
7. LOVE YOUR CHOICE OF COLORS.
8. THANKS FOR THE DRINK.
9. YOU REALLY CAN DANCE.
10. WHAT A MEMORY!
11. WHAT A NEAT DRESS!
12. I'M HAPPY YOU HELPED ME OUT.
13. YOU DID A LOT OF WORK THIS WEEK.
14. WOW! YOU MAKE IT LOOK EASY.
15. LOVE THE PASS YOU THREW.
16. WHAT BEAUTIFUL DRAPRIES.
17. YOUR SPELLING IS IMPROVING NICELY.
18. YOU ARE A THINKER.
19. YOU SURE CAN HIT THE BALL.
20. LOVE YOUR CHOICE OF RESTAURANTS.
21. YOU SURE HANDLED THAT CLASS WELL.
22. WISH I COULD MEET PEOPLE LIKE YOU DO.
23. THANKS FOR LISTENING.
24. I FEEL LUCKY THAT I'VE GOT A DAD LIKE YOU.
25. YOU'RE GETTING FASTER AT YOUR JOB EVERY DAY.
26. I WISH I HAD YOUR HAIR.
27. YOU'VE GOT YOUR BRAIN IN GEAR TODAY.
28. I REALLY ENJOY BEING WITH YOU.
29. YOU MAKE PEOPLE FEEL AT EASE.
30. LOVE THE YOU WRITE.
31. YOU SURE HAVE DETERMINATION.
32. LOVE THE WAY YOU TREAT YOUR KIDS.
33. I LOVE YOUR HONESTY.

activities, e.g., "I like the way you cut the grass." On the preceding page are 33 ways to give warm fuzzies.

Remember the Type A personality? Society rewards type A behavior in children. Try to be creative and think of warm fuzzies that reward the process and not the product, e.g., not — "You produced a good report card," but, "It looks like you have been trying very hard to do your best." Remember to reduce stress, you aim the warm fuzzies at "Being" instead of "Doing." A mother could say, "Johnny, I sure like the way you got along with your friend today." Aiming warm fuzzies at "cooperation qualities" rather than competitive qualities will go a long way toward preventing the mass production of Type A personalities and increase the Type B philosophers who like themselves well enough to take time to "stop and smell the roses."

Power of warm fuzzies

Bill has a doctorate in psychology and teaches "self-image" psychology. I heard him tell the story of how he got into the field. In the sixth grade he had a teacher who gave "warm fuzzies". Regularly, she would look for the good things kids had done and let them know with a warm fuzzy. Bill was in the slow group, but his teacher noticed his alert mind and said, "Bill you sure are a quick thinker." Bill finished high school and went to work on the railroad. He had no challenge in his job. His thoughts went back to his sixth grade teacher and he remembered her saying, "Bill, you have an alert mind." He thought about it. "She is right," he said, "I need a challenge." Today Bill teaches self-concept psychology at a university in Florida because of the warm fuzzies of one sixth-grade teacher.

I personally had a similar experience. In 1972, I had lunch with Gordon, a friend of mine, who is in real estate. He said, "Jim, I've been to communication workshops all over the country. Your class is better." (A warm fuzzy.) "When are you going to leave the schools and go into the communication business?" A year later when Aurora schools refused to grant me a half-time contract, I said, "Maybe Gordon was right." In 1973, Fran and I started Communications Unlimited.

The thought just occured to me. If it hadn't been for Gordon's warm fuzzy, I would still be a school counselor. I wouldn't be sitting here writing **B.S. and Live Longer**. If this book helps you, thank Gordon, who started the ball rolling.

III. The adult - adult approach

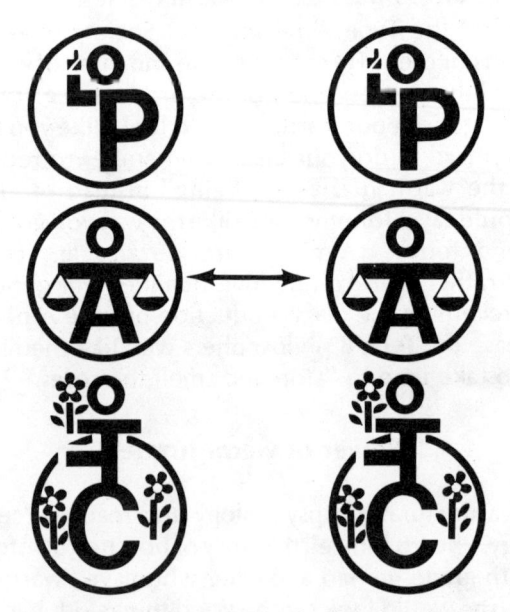

About two years, ago, a young high school teacher came to class at the spring quarter. She had been teaching high school for three years. She was about to throw in the towel on teaching. During the period of the semester class, she assessed her problem. She clearly saw that her approach was the critical parent-child one concerning her attitude of "shape up or ship out." This approach created stress in the kids. The kids reduced it in creative ways like painting "I love you teacher" on her car. The next year she switched to an adult-adult approach and wrote, "I can't believe the difference. It is like night and day. I've learned to relax and like the kids and they relax and like me. We still get the job done, but we have fun while doing it."

1. Sell instead of tell

There are a number of ways to create an adult-adult relationship. One way is to "sell and not tell." To sell ideas to kids, give them a share in the decision making. Bill, a good friend of mine, has five children and is a neat teacher. While his kids were growing up, he ran the "family circle." Every week they had a share in what went on in the family. They would decide such things as where to go on vacations or on weekends. He said that giving them a share in decisions gave them a sense of belonging, worth, and independence.

Create as many choices as possible, e.g., "Johnny, do you want to go swimming or take in a movie?" The item of choice may not be monumental, but giving the child the choice of doing what he wants to do is one of the major stress-reducing tools.

Young students or little children can't verbalize the stress caused by parents or teachers who never think of giving children or students choices. Most college teachers assigned term papers as if this were the only infallible method of education. They gave no choice. Listen to Sandy's reaction and stress reducing letter.

Dear Jim,

I have always wanted to begin a letter with a P.S. This shall be the letter that I do it in!

P.S.

I don't like to write! I don't like to write! I don't like to write anything at all, fat or thin, long or short!

I have always wanted to tell an instructor how much I don't like to write! In college I would pray that just one of my teachers would discover what I had learned by some other means than those Damn!!! term papers. But each in turn would say write a few million-paged term paper and they always caused me hour upon hour of pain and worry.

I don't like to write — let me draw pictures, cut out pictures, collect thoughts or best of all let me share my ideas and thoughts with you, by talking face to face. When will they learn that there are other ways of learning and sharing what you have learned besides term papers. I would like to go to a class and have a part in the decision as to what we will do for a final.

I have finally shared this with someone. Thanks for being you and being here.

Sandy

2. The "suds" level approach

Use the STANDARD UNIT OF DISCOMFORT SCALE, nicknamed "SUDS". It goes from one to one hundred. Families as well as classes could do regular SUDS LEVEL checks as a means of keeping an ever present outlet or safety valve for stress overload. Here's an example.

I used the SUDS LEVEL at the very beginning of a government seminar. I explained that the higher level up to 100 is the uptight level, and the lower level is the relaxed level. I asked four people to write their SUDS LEVEL on the board. They scored rather high: 75, 82, 87, and 91. The anxiety of a new class raised their SUDS LEVEL. At the end of the day, these same people retook the SUDS LEVEL test. All of them were below the 25% mark. The interaction activities and the relaxed classroom atmosphere reduced the SUDS LEVEL. Learning to check out the SUDS LEVEL, either your own or those you work with, is a wonderful way to reduce stress.

3. Listening

A third and dynamic way to create adult-adult communication is by listening to kids. Listening is a splendid way of saying, "I care." It tells them that you love them. For children, the feeling of being loved, is the greatest stress reducer.

Telephone call to Judy

The other night I returned a call to Marilyn, a long time friend. Her little girl answered the phone and I asked to speak to Marilyn. She said, "My mommy is not home, but my daddy is. Do you want to talk to him?" I said, "Later, how about if I talk to you first?" I asked her name, age, and we talked about things she liked most to do. We had a real interesting talk. The next day Marilyn called. She said, "My little Judy was super high all day because you took the time to talk with her on the phone. Most people don't."

Two reactions to mud

We tend to yell at kids instead of listening to them.

I can't help but think of Mrs. X. Her little boy brought his truck filled with mud inside the house. She yelled, "Billy, get that truck out of here. Don't you have any brains? If you spill any mud on my carpet you will go without supper." That same night she had a cocktail party. In walked Mr. Smith. Guess what? He walked in the same mud Billy had put into his truck. What a vastly different reaction. "Mr. Smith, you may want to wipe your shoes on these newspapers," she gently sugggested. She did not yell, "Mr. Smith, if you walk on my rug with that mud, you'll get no cocktails tonight." Incidents like this are daily occurrences. We still treat kids as "non-persons."

Artistic listening

Kids, just like big people, have uppers and downers. I frequently have my little boys draw an upper-downer drawing of the day so they don't collect gray stamps (the words they use for stress). These drawings are from Kevy and Kenny.

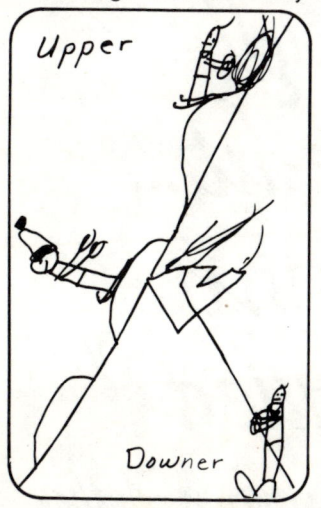

Here's Kevy's explanation. "Going skiing with my Daddy's a real upper. I really have a good time. The kite is a downer because it broke and I couldn't fly it any more.

Kenny's explanation was, "The upper is playing cars on Mommy's waterbed. What a ball! The downer is the Donald Duck picture. Kevy got a Snoopy picture as a surprise and I got Donald Duck. I got cheated because I wanted Snoopy."

Their uppers and downers are not monumental in our eyes, but these things are important to them. What is significant is that

"A Child is a candle to be lit... not a cup to be filled"

— unknown Author

these little boys are learning to get their good and bad feelings out through "artistic listening."

4. Exploring type B values

A fourth way to help children explore their values and get to know themselves, is to ask the following: a. "What is your goal for this year?" b. "What is the biggest challenge in being a boy or in being a girl?" c. "What is your motto?" d. "What really brings you fulfillment in life?" Notice, these are the Type B philosophy questions that hopefully will get them to think about who they are and what they want out of life. In my book, **Having Fun Being Yourself**, there are a number of other ways to help children explore their values.

5. Creating a "free to be" atmosphere

The fifth and hardest way, especially for parents, is to let your child be himself. I've met so many people in all walks of life who are what they are because their parents chose it. "Well, mom and dad always wanted me to be a teacher. I don't really want it, but it's too late now." This often begins with Little League. How many kids play little league football because that is what their parents want. Loads of parents are still trying to live their kid's lives. Listen to the real case of Rich. This is happening in my neighborhood. I got the inside story from Alice, the mother of the girl Rich is going steady with.

Alice writes: "His Dad wants him to be a Denver Bronco. Rich doesn't like football. He is on a college football scholarship. His Dad told him not to come home if he doesn't intend to play four years of football. This summer Rich intends to come back to Denver from his college in Texas. He plans to get an apartment, support himself and make it on his own without football. His father wants to live two lives, his own and his son's."

His father is raising his children according to his own values instead of creating an atmosphere in which children can be free to become themselves. Letting the children become the artists of their own personality is a monumental way to shut down a stress generator in child rearing.

6. Child - proofing

The sixth way is to child-proof things. If possible have a kids' room without a lot of high-value fragile decorations and expensive lamps. Kids don't generally place a premium on a hundred dollar statue, so don't put it in the kid-proof area.

A friend tells the story of the parents who are good at the child-proofing approach. When they go on a trip, they let their two kids paint in the back seat. They cover the car seat with oil cloth in case some paint falls. Isn't that so much better than telling them "to shut up" or "act like grownups." For this trip the kids were busy painting and the parents had a relaxing talk. High stress was prevented by the foresight of child-proofing the trip.

7. Being transparent (owning your feelings)

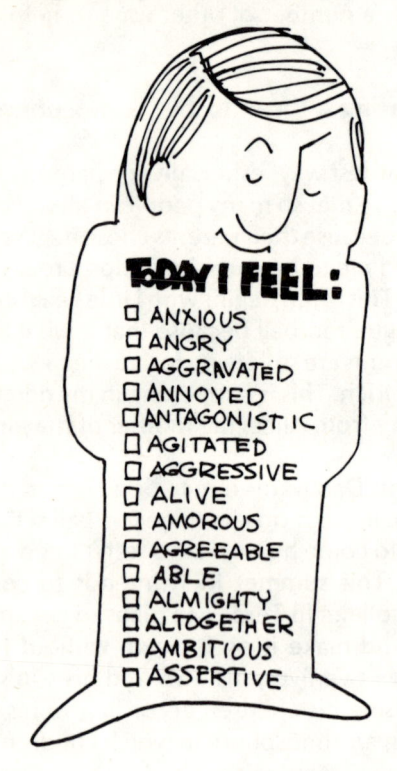

TODAY I FEEL:
- ANXIOUS
- ANGRY
- AGGRAVATED
- ANNOYED
- ANTAGONISTIC
- AGITATED
- AGGRESSIVE
- ALIVE
- AMOROUS
- AGREEABLE
- ABLE
- ALMIGHTY
- ALTOGETHER
- AMBITIOUS
- ASSERTIVE

The seventh way to operate out of the adult-adult is to be open and honest, be transparent so the students (if you are a teacher) or the children know exactly how you feel. More stress in the world of work is created by supervisors who don't know how to be transparent.

I remember Martin telling me, "I've had more stress in my new job in six months than I had in five years under my former boss. This new boss never says anything about anything. I don't know whether he likes me, my work or anything else . . . Hell, I don't even like my job anymore."

Teachers and parents in a way are supervisors of children. If you don't learn to own your feelings and become transparent, your kids are going to have just as much stress as Martin is having on his job.

How do you own your feeling? It can be in two simple steps. First, state what you are feeling; using the words "I feel." Secondly, describe the behavior that causes the feeling. For instance, if you are upset because your child is late for supper, you can own your feelings by saying, "Billy, I really get anxious when you are late for supper and do not call and tell me." That is much better than saying, "Billy, you drive me crazy with your lateness. You are growing up just like your old man"

Learning to own your own feelings will make you a transparent teacher or parent. This transparency will go a long way in reducing stress in your students or your children.

8. Teaching children to cope with killer statements

In order to teach children how to deal with killer statements, we have to take a stand against them ourselves. For instance, if you saw a child being physically beat up by another, would you not intervene to stop it? Why not take the same stand when one kid is beating the hell out of the other's self-image?

One teacher I knew took a definite and transparent stand on self-image killers. He would say, "As a teacher, I feel strongly that we have a few extremely important rules in this class. My most important one is that I cannot stand killer statements, they ruin my day. When anyone uses them, I'll be transparent and quickly let you know."

Taking a stand against killer statements is a stress reducer of the highest magnitude. One of the biggest stress generators among children is in the vicious form of children putting down other children. I would like to reinforce this with several examples.

The killer in the whirlpool

About a year ago Kevin and Kenny, my two little boys, were in a hotel swimming pool. They decided they wanted to take a whirlpool so they left. Before long they were back and said that they didn't like the whirlpool because there was a mean teenage girl in there. I decided to take a whirlpool to assess the situation. This teenager had her two little sisters with her and she was shouting out killer statements as fast as a soldier could fire a machine gun. "Shut up . . . Stop it . . . You dummy" . . . etc. I decided to interrupt her rapid fire and said, "I really feel sorry for your two little sisters when you treat them like that." She said, "Well, that's how my mom and dad talk to me."

So kids learn "put downs" or "killer statements" from their parents. I guess it goes all the way back to Adam and Eve. Eve said, "Eat that apple and eat it now." Adam was under so much stress that he ate them out of house and home.

Joan's example

Joan is a super person and a friend of mine. She is also an expert in special education. She has really seen how the special ed kids suffer under the vicious fire of killer statements. Schools tried to meet the needs of special ed kids and needed to classify them. They tried using nice sounding classifications like "learning disabled," "perceptually handicapped," "slow learner," but regardless of euphemistic symbols, the term "special education" is often viewed as a "put down". It is a place to put "odd" children who don't belong in society or in a regular school class.

Joan Kendall sums it up so well in her poem.

"I'm here," he cried
They did not see.
He can't belong.
Just let him be.

"I'm a child," he said.
They did not hear.
He was apart,
Something to fear.

"I'm a boy," he spoke.
They turned away.

He did not join,
He did not play.

*"I'm alone," he sighed.
"My name is Fred.
No, just a kid
From Special Ed."*

Someone once said that "children are the cruelest to one another." They don't want to be, but don't know how to remedy the situation. The parent or teacher taking a stand against killer statements creates an atmosphere that kids want and need. Lisa, a mother of four children, tried it and here is what she writes. The results are amazing. "My kids know the house rule, NO KILLER STATEMENTS. The neighbor kids caught on quick and like it. It took a few months, but it was worth it. When I hear a 'You dum-dum' I simply come out with the adult-adult approach of saying what I feel. 'I really get upset when I hear you using put-down statements.' I'm transparent on that. In fact, sometimes we talk about how to communicate their feelings without killer statements. It turned out to be wonderful."

One thing for sure, it has reduced stress in myself because I don't have to listen to killer statements which used to hurt me as much as the kids.

. . . Jim took it a step further

Some weeks ago I had a principal of an elementary school in my class. In his school he has reduced discipline trips to the office by 90% just by teaching teachers and children to own their own feelings. He teaches kids to cope effectively with killer statements by showing them how to own their own feelings. One little first-grader was afraid to ride the bus because the older kids teased him. The prinicipal engaged in an adult-adult communication with him exploring why the older kids would do that. They came up with the conclusion that they don't do it to hurt him, but to attempt to put themselves up by putting others down. The next time it happened the little first-grader said: "I really feel bad when you call me those names." It worked for this little kid and many others. The stress level of this whole elementary school is at a low level because so many are able to cope with "put downs" by owning their own feelings.

9. The need to rebel

The last adult-adult approach is "last but not least." It is communicating with reality. The reality is that kids have the NEED to rebel. Ditching school is one way to express it. In my day it was drinking booze. Today it is booze or pot. Don Shaw is super with teenagers. He says if parents recognized this adult-adult approach to reality, namely, that kids have to have their needs fulfilled, they would reduce a lot of stress within. "When I was teaching, I would always have some rule that I knew the kids would break. It really worked. It fulfilled their need to rebel and it didn't bother me because I didn't expect them to keep it. Stress was reduced for all concerned. If we as parents don't provide something to fulfill this need to rebel, the kids might fulfill it in more dangerous or destructive ways." Don really has a helpful insight. Every normal adult went through some form of rebellion, e.g., playing hookey, smoking in the high school johns, sneaking out at night or sneaking into a movie. The adult approach to this reality is a fantastic stress reducer.

IV. The child - child approach

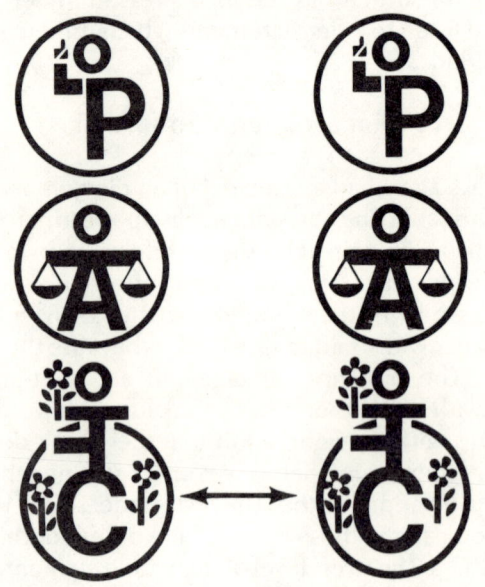

If we can learn anything from kids, it is how to use our child part of our "You, Inc." Losing touch with the creative, wholesome, fun-loving, child-part of our personality is a stress disaster. Making use of our child part of our "You, Inc." is a good outlet for stress.

Along this line, isn't it ironic that in all my research of the various authors on stress, I found little or no part of the fun-loving child? Stress is serious, but there has to be a humorous side of everything. Since humor is one of the stress reducers, wouldn't it seem fitting that the stress writers would sprinkle their writings with some fun things so people could relax and reduce stress as they learn about the tools to do so?

How much time do you think the average parent actually plays with the children? Unfortunately, but true, most of the communication is parent-child both at home and in school. I recommend just taking 20 minutes a day actually operating out of your child with your children.

Cory uses the child - child approach at home

Cory tried it. "Dear Jim, I thought I would give this 20 minute child thing a whirl. My boys are five and seven. Every night when I come home from work, I try the '20 minute child-time.' At first I felt silly playing cars and playing hide and go seek. Then I began to discover how creative and humorous my kids were. It was fascinating. I was in a whole new world. It became fun for me. I learned a lot. Now I look forward to my child-time and often it goes way beyond the 20 minutes. I was missing a whole world of beautiful experiences until I stepped into this child-child approach. It is more relaxing than the cocktails I used to unwind with after work." I know what Cory means. I also love to spend time "child to child" with my two little boys.

Using the child-child in the classroom

Joyce was teaching a class on marriage in a rather large suburban high school. In the question and answer period at the end George asked: "Do infants have more fun in infancy than adults do in adultery." The class snickered. Joyce, could have come back out of the critical-parent part of her "You, Inc." saying: "George, this is not funny. One more remark and you will go to the principal." Instead she recognized that George was speaking from the child part of his "George, Inc.", so she responded from her child. "George, there hasn't been too much research on that subject. Maybe you would want to do a house to house survey on the question and give a report to the class." The class laughed, and stress was reduced. In Joyce's class, the kids can learn and have fun at the same time because she has versatility in her communication. She can operate child-to-child as well as adult-adult.

V. Does your "cope" runneth over with stress?

If you are a teacher or a parent and your 'cope' runneth over, I'll bet you a dollar to a donut that you, like most adults, are using the critical-parent (so called "discipline approach") with your children. This approach is a tremendous GENERATOR OF STRESS for you and your children. If you want to be able to keep your "stress cope" from overflowing, try the alternate approaches in communicating with students or children, e.g., the adult-adult, the child-child, or the nurturing parent-child.

Two years ago, I had Karen in my class. She was a high school teacher who, after three years of teaching, was looking for a job outside of education. During the class she analyzed her communication. Listen to her letter.

Dear Jim
It didn't take me long to see that I was communicating with teenagers just like my parents and my teachers communicated with me, i.e., critical-parent child. This year I switched mainly to adult-adult with some child-child. I have reduced my stress level by 300%. I no longer hate my job. I love it. I wish I could have learned how to communicate with students in college.
  Sincerely,
  Karen

Knowing how to communicate in ways other than the critical parent or the "I'm okay, you're not okay" approach will, in my view, definitely control the communication stress generator. This is not an ivory tower theory. In the last twenty years, I've worked with school children, especially teenagers. I received a great deal of satisfaction and very little stress. It works for me and for many others . . . try it, and you may like it.

VI. Changing the thing you can change

What better way to wind up this communication generator special than to center on the one thing we definitely can change, "ourselves". We have walked down the communication aisle of our supermarket by exploring the variety of tools. Now let's step back into the world of our attitudes and see if "role-switching" can enhance our view of our students or children.

Switching roles

Thousands of children die in accidents every year. Switching yourself into the role of those parents who have lost a child will increase your appreciation level of your own children.

John Gunther wrote **Death Be Not Proud**, about their son's 15 month fight to live. In the epilogue his mother implores those who still have sons and daughters to embrace them with a little added rapture and keener awareness of joy. Loss really creates appreciation.

A five minute loss role-switch

I spent five minutes in the role of a parent who lost a boy. I feel I've always loved children but my appreciation has been enriched by a five minute loss. One day while I was working on my car, Kevin came running over half-soaked. He was only four and all he said was, "Kenny is still in the stream." I ran to the park and the little stream was now a rushing river. Someone in the mountains had opened the dike by mistake. For five minutes I thought Kenny had drowned. Then he came walking from the other end of the park. I rushed to grab him and hug him. It was a resurrection from the dead for me.

Talk about stress, it took me two years before I could even talk about the incident without getting choked up or crying. Maybe this incident accounts for my high level appreciation of our two little boys. My boys are about 10% stressors, but 90% stress reducers.

It works for us

Fran and I found the things (outlined in this chapter) have worked for us in creating a low stress atmosphere in which our children have the space to become themselves. It has really been so rewarding to hear people spontaneously say, "Your kids seem so comfortable and free to be." So far, this approach has really worked. Who knows, they might turn out to be modern day "Jesse James's" but right now, these things seem to be working.

A low stress marriage is at the core

I almost got married at 18 and it would have been a high stress marriage because I didn't know myself or anyone else. When I got married at 37, I was looking for someone who liked children and was an accepting and a flexible person who would give me room or space to be myself. I've been married for nine years and I won't say I lucked out because I got what I was looking for. Fran lets me be me and I let her be her. In that relationship there is little stress. I think this is what creates the low stress level in which the children feel free to be themselves.

That brings us back to the golden axiom of the philosophers, "You can't give what you don't have." Don't collect stress as a parent or teacher and you won't give it to your kids. If anything sums it up, it is the following poem. (Permission granted, John Phillip Co., Campbell, Calif., poem by Dorothy Law Nolte.)

CHILDREN LEARN WHAT THEY LIVE

If a child lives with criticism, He learns to condemn.

If a child lives with hostility, He learns to fight.

If a child lives with ridicule, He learns to be shy.

If a child lives with shame, He learns to feel guilty.

If a child lives with tolerance, He learns to be patient.

If a child lives with encouragement, He learns confidence.

If a child lives with praise, He learns to appreciate.

If a child lives with fairness, He learns justice.

If a child lives with security, He learns to have faith.

If a child lives with approval, He learns to like himself.

If a child lives with acceptance and friendship,
He learns to find love in the world.

APPENDIX II

The following letter sums up the beautiful experience when a person identifies and copes effectively with a stress generator in their life. Approximately one year ago, Mary, depressed and bewildered, showed up in my stress class as a result of reading **Re-entry Into The Single Life.** Today, one year later, she wrote this beautiful letter. Here it is.

Dear Jim,

It was 10 years ago as I was preparing to rig my boat to sail when along came a fine ship and a very attractive captain. Instead of him helping me with my boat, he decided he would sail it for me. I being an inexperienced sailor agreed to this arrangement for many years until I noticed that whenever I desired to sail for new horizons or different ports that I thought would be interesting, the captain pulled rank and so we sailed his plotted course. As I crewed on my own ship over the years, I began to think, "Life holds no joy for me." I felt I no longer had any pride in my ship or in my ability to sail it. The responsibility of his ship growing heavier and the added burden of mine became annoying to him. I concluded that I had three choices. I could sail the captain's chartered course, jump overboard out of frustration, or I could sail my own ship come hell or high water. The very idea of me sailing my own ship infuriated the captain, he thinking me incapable. Being a lover of a good book, I wasn't about to jump overboard during the third chapter and never know how the story ended. So came the hell or high water decision. I might add that it is not easy to mutiny on your own ship. But I convinced the captain that my ship was sinking and he best get off and so he did. My ship, my ship, it was in dire need of repair from bow to stern, from keel to mast. I surveyed the situation through salt watered eyes. It was a sturdy ship I thought. Well crafted. The hulls were in great shape and the sails would do for now. A new coat of paint, a new block here, replace a cleat there, and sailing lessons couldn't hurt. I had my friends help me repair my ship, and the sailing classes gave me a new confidence I'd never known before. As I gained strength an unconscious thought came to me, "God I hope I have enough time left to see and do all I've dreamed for." I don't plan to sail my ship all by myself forever for I need someone to share my adventures with. I don't need a captain for I am the captain. I dont need a crew for I have a crew until he's old enough to be his own captain. I need a skipper who is the captain *of his own ship. We will be each other's co-captains. Together we can weather any storm. So thanks to you, Jim, God, and myself, I have now left the harbor and the whole ocean lies before me.*

Mary

Through participation in the Stress Reduction class, Mary came from near shipwreck to a happy and fulfilled Captain of Her Own Ship.

All the materials in the class that she used to rebuild her ship are in the covers of this book. Hopefully, you too can make use of them to beat stress and live fuller, happier, and longer.

Reactions to Stress Workshops

Mary Jean Vitolo - Primary teacher — *"What I learned in the stress workshop I was able to use with my students immediately."*

Sally Clemens - Sales Representative — *"This seminar has helped tremendously in coping with the stress of a competitive world."*

Kathy Clark - Avon manager — *"Your workshop has reduced stress and added fun to my work."*

Ely Gamon - Fire Department Officer — *"The Value of this workshop is more than money can buy. I've reassessed my whole life."*

Jan Skiff - Government Secretary — *"I've lost 15 pounds since this workshop. I've learned other outlets for stress instead of eating."*

Bill Benson - Real Estate Broker — *"This stress workshop made me aware of how much of a Type A personality I am. I've now begun to acquire Type B behaviors and I'm going to beat stress and live longer."*

Louise Glass - Yoga Instructor — *"Yoga has always reduced stress for me. Your seminar made me identify my major stress generator. Learning to cope with it has reduced loads of stress in my life."*

Tom Bailey - Business Executive — *"I wasn't even aware of any stress in my life until I volunteered for the bio-feedback demonstration. That was a real eye opener. As a result of this course I am making significant changes in my life. The business world needs relevant courses like this one."*

Books you may find helpful

Dr. Hans, Selye, **"Stress Without Distress"**

W. Suojanen and D. Hudson, **"Coping With Stress and Addictive Work Behavior"**

Wayne Oates, **"Confessions of a Workaholic"**

Meyer Friedman, and Ray Rosenman, **"Type A Behavior and Your Heart"**

T. H. Holmes and R. H. Rahe, "The Social Readjustment Rating Scale," **Journal of Psychosomatic Research**

John Garquhar, "Stress and How to Cope With It" **(Stanford Magazine,** Fall-Winter, (1977)

Sidney Simon, L. Howe, and H. Kirschenbaum, **"Values Clarification"**

James Lynch, **"The Broken Heart"**

Herbert Benson, "Your Innate Asset For Combating Stress" **Harvard Business Review,** July, August, 1974

Dr. Jim Keelan, **"Having Fun Being Yourself"**

Dr. Jim Keelan, **"Re-entry Into the Single Life"**

John Gunther, **"Death Be Not Proud"**

Muriel James and Dorothy Jongeward, **"Born to Win"**

Phippil Zimbardo and Addison Westley, **"Shyness"**

Trina Paulus, **"Hope for the Flowers"**

Ashley Montagu, **"Touching, the Human Significance of the Skin"**

Alvyn Freed, **"T. A. for Tots"**

Marguerite Michaels, "Our Nation's Teachers Are Taking a Beating" **(Rocky Mountain News -** February, 1978)

Herbert Benson, **"The Relaxation Response"**

Micki Siegel, "The Everyday Unending Stress of Being a Cop" **(Rocky Mountain News, Parade Section,** March 12, 1978)

Thomas Gordon, **"Parent Effectiveness Training"**

Antonie de Saint Exuper, **"The Little Prince"**

Sidney Jourard, **"The Transparent Self"**

Merill Harmin, **"How to Get Rid of Emotions That Give a Pain in The Neck"**

COMMUNICATIONS UNLIMITED

Originally organized to strengthen "YOU, INC."

SCOPE: The purpose of **Communications Unlimited** is to help people know who they are, to be themselves, and to attain a more fulfilled life, through learning creative communication skills.

The concept of **Communications Unlimited** is the art of communicating **beyond words.** It is the ability of making another person aware that you are sharing his/her feelings. It is openness within the realm of reality.

THREE BOOKS TO COPE WITH STRESS

Jim Keelan writes for "YOU, INC."
"Nobody says it better."

1. **THE WORLD OF STRESS**

   B-1 B.S.* & Live Longer: *(Beat Stress) August, 1978. This is a creative approach to coping with stress. Backed with strong research, the book quotes hard statistics which are complemented by first hand testimonials around stress experiences. The major focus is on stopping up the **Stress Generators** as well as identifying tools and techniques for **Stress Reduction.** $4.95

2. **A MAJOR STRESS GENERATOR FOR MANY.**

   B-2 Re-Entry into the Single Life: 1977. The book addresses the chaos of guilt and fears experienced by the divorced and the widowed. The author guides the reader through three steps, aiming toward achieving the status of being a complete person and removing the barriers to future relationships. $4.95

3. **A MAJOR STRESS GENERATOR FOR EVERYONE.**

   B-3 Having Fun Being Yourself: 1975. This book was written to help YOU get to know and to like YOU. There is an orderly progression toward recognizing your values and identifying as either a "cupfiller" or a "candlelighter." The author addresses truth . . . the kinds of truth that will make you free to have fun being yourself. $4.95

WORKSHOPS FOR LIVING

*One Day or One Week - Scheduled for your needs.
(Full information on content, format, costs on request)*

W-1 Stress Reduction Through Effective Communication
W-2 Effective Communication
W-3 Time Management
W-4 Effective Goal Setting
W-5 Effective Listening and Name Recall
W-6 Problem Solving/Conflict Resolution
W-7 Motivation of Low-Skilled Employees
W-8 Are You a Part Time Woman in a Full Time World?
W-9 Personal Values in Today's World
W-10 Coping with Drug Abuse and Alcoholism
W-11 Communication for Secretaries
W-12 Women in the Middle
W-13 Take Me Along Hawaii! Vacationing and Learning in the Heart of Waikiki
W-14 Building Bridges for Better Communication
W-15 Coping with Life Styles and Work Styles
W-16 "Make those Miracles Happen" Motivation

TAPES TO COPE WITH STRESS

T-1	The Hidden Stress Generator	$5.95
T-2	On The Job Stress Generator	$5.95
T-3	You May Be The Cause of Your Own Stress	$5.95
T-4	The Three Phase Stress-Coping Tool	$5.95
T-5	The Personal Stress Test	$5.95
T-6	Stress Reducing Techniques	$5.95

TEST DISTRIBUTORS

PT-1 The Personal Profile System — A Plan to Understand Self and Others. $5.00 each $400.00 per C

PT-2 The Job Factor Analysis System — "A View of Your Job"
                    $3.00 each $250.00 per C

ORDER FORM

To: Communications Unlimited
   Division of Distribution
   7057 Wright Ct.
   Arvada, CO 80004

Please send information on the workshops checked below:

☐ W-1   ☐ W-2   ☐ W-3   ☐ W-4   ☐ W-5
☐ W-6   ☐ W-7   ☐ W-8   ☐ W-9   ☐ W-10
☐ W-11 ☐ W-12 ☐ W-13 ☐ W-14 ☐ W-15
☐ W-16

Check is enclosed for $ _____ for the items checked below.

BOOKS: ☐ B-1   ☐ B-2   ☐ B-3

TESTS: ☐ PT-1 _____   ☐ PT-2 _____ (specify quantity)

TAPES: ☐ T-1   ☐ T-2   ☐ T-3   ☐ T-4
☐ T-5   ☐ T-6

Stress Dots: ☐ SD-1 _____ (specify quantity)
                        4/$1.00

☐ S-1   B.S. and Live Longer T-shirts
☐ S-2   Having Fun Being Yourself T-shirts
        S:30-34   M:38-40   L:42-44
              $6.00 each

(Add $.75 for postage and handling)

Name _____

Address _____

City/State/Zip _____

Telephone _____
